Christen Brown

Hand Embroidery

DICTIONARY

500+ Stitches

Tips, Techniques & Design Ideas

C&T PUBLISHING

Text copyright © 2021 by Christen Brown

Photography and artwork copyright © 2021 by C&T Publishing, Inc.

Publisher: Amy Barrett-Daffin

Creative Director: Gailen Runge

Acquisitions Editor: Roxane Cerda

Managing Editor: Liz Aneloski

Editor: Karla Menaugh

Technical Editor: Helen Frost

Cover/Book Designer: April Mostek

Production Coordinator: Tim Manibusan

Production Editor: Jennifer Warren

Illustrator: Linda Johnson

Photo Assistant: Lauren Herberg

Photography by Estefany Gonzalez and Lauren Herberg of
C&T Publishing, Inc., unless otherwise noted

Published by C&T Publishing, Inc., P.O. Box 1456, Lafayette, CA 94549

Library of Congress Cataloging-in-Publication Data

Names: Brown, Christen (Christen Joan) author.

Title: Hand embroidery dictionary : 500+ stitches; tips, techniques &
design ideas / Christen Brown.

Description: Lafayette, CA : C&T Publishing, [2021] | Includes
bibliographical references.

Identifiers: LCCN 2021020630 | ISBN 9781644030097 (trade
paperback) | ISBN 9781644030103 (ebook)

Subjects: LCSH: Embroidery. | Embroidery--Terminology. |
Stitches (Sewing)

Classification: LCC TT770 .B88773 2021 | DDC 746.44--dc23

LC record available at https://lccn.loc.gov/2021020630

Printed in the USA

10 9 8 7 6 5 4 3 2

SPECIAL ACKNOWLEDGMENTS

I have been fortunate to have the most wonderful people
helping me throughout the process of designing, writing,
editing, and photographing this book. I would like to thank
each and every person whose expertise has touched these
pages. Special thanks go to Liz and Roxane, who have been
there from the start. You know how special you are, and I
do appreciate you.

My special thanks go to the Colonial Needle Company for
providing the needles and Finca perle cotton that were
used in the samples for the embroidery stitch dictionary
and many of the gallery pieces.

Blue Bird Nest

MY BIGGEST FANS

To my husband, Kevin, and daughter, Gwen—thank you for your unconditional love and support and for allowing me to play in my room. Love you both to the moon and back!

Mushroom Garden

HAPPY CREATING

I dedicate this book to all of my students: past, present, and future. Thank you for giving me this opportunity to share my knowledge with you. May you always find the time to enjoy the creative adventure.
—*Christen*

Sea Urchins

Contents

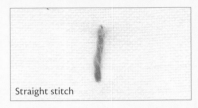
Straight stitch

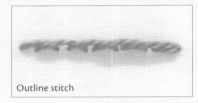
Outline stitch

Whip-stitch star

Lazy daisy stitch

Chain stitch

Barb stitch

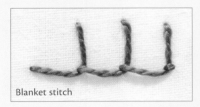
Blanket stitch

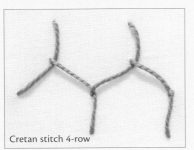

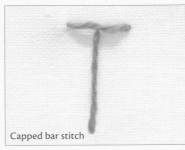
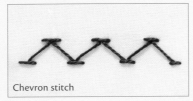

Visual Guide

The Visual Guide is meant to be a quick reference for you, the reader. The stitches are arranged mostly in alphabetical order under each stitch family.

STRAIGHT STITCHES (page 43)

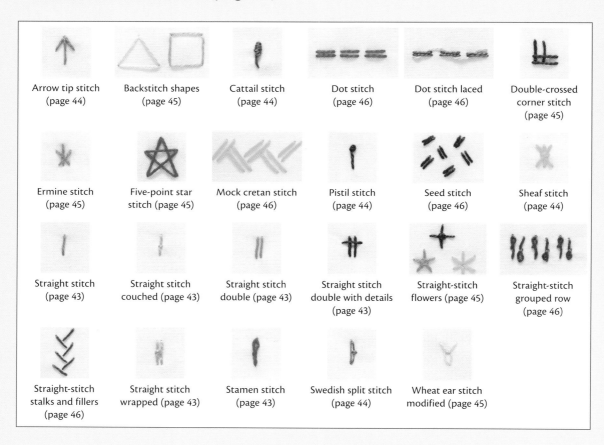

Arrow tip stitch
(page 44)

Backstitch shapes
(page 45)

Cattail stitch
(page 44)

Dot stitch
(page 46)

Dot stitch laced
(page 46)

Double-crossed
corner stitch
(page 45)

Ermine stitch
(page 45)

Five-point star
stitch (page 45)

Mock cretan stitch
(page 46)

Pistil stitch
(page 44)

Seed stitch
(page 46)

Sheaf stitch
(page 44)

Straight stitch
(page 43)

Straight stitch
couched (page 43)

Straight stitch
double (page 43)

Straight stitch
double with details
(page 43)

Straight-stitch
flowers (page 45)

Straight-stitch
grouped row
(page 46)

Straight-stitch
stalks and fillers
(page 46)

Straight stitch
wrapped (page 43)

Stamen stitch
(page 43)

Swedish split stitch
(page 44)

Wheat ear stitch
modified (page 45)

OUTLINE STITCHES (page 47)

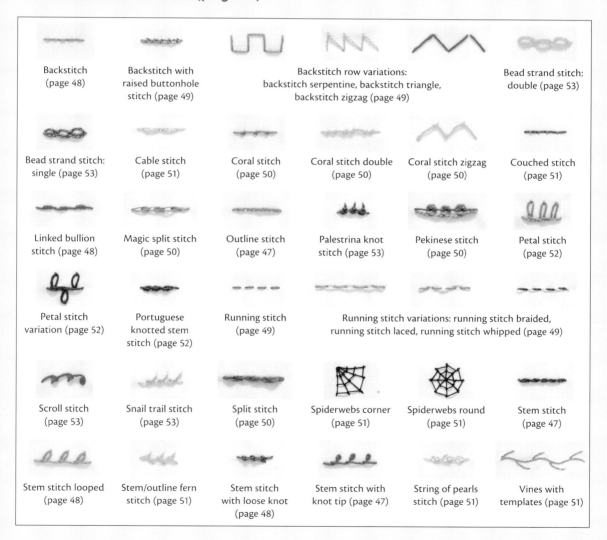

Backstitch (page 48)	Backstitch with raised buttonhole stitch (page 49)

Backstitch row variations: backstitch serpentine, backstitch triangle, backstitch zigzag (page 49)

Bead strand stitch: double (page 53)

Bead strand stitch: single (page 53)

Cable stitch (page 51)

Coral stitch (page 50)

Coral stitch double (page 50)

Coral stitch zigzag (page 50)

Couched stitch (page 51)

Linked bullion stitch (page 48)

Magic split stitch (page 50)

Outline stitch (page 47)

Palestrina knot stitch (page 53)

Pekinese stitch (page 50)

Petal stitch (page 52)

Petal stitch variation (page 52)

Portuguese knotted stem stitch (page 52)

Running stitch (page 49)

Running stitch variations: running stitch braided, running stitch laced, running stitch whipped (page 49)

Scroll stitch (page 53)

Snail trail stitch (page 53)

Split stitch (page 50)

Spiderwebs corner (page 51)

Spiderwebs round (page 51)

Stem stitch (page 47)

Stem stitch looped (page 48)

Stem/outline fern stitch (page 51)

Stem stitch with loose knot (page 48)

Stem stitch with knot tip (page 47)

String of pearls stitch (page 51)

Vines with templates (page 51)

KNOTTED, WOVEN, AND WHIPPED STITCHES (page 54)

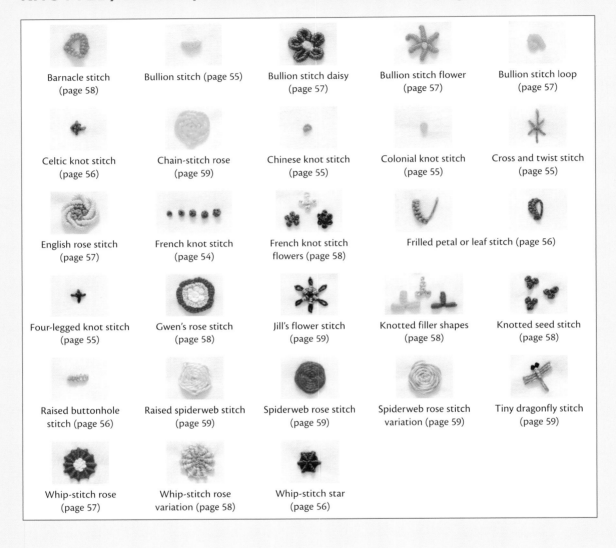

Barnacle stitch
(page 58)

Bullion stitch (page 55)

Bullion stitch daisy
(page 57)

Bullion stitch flower
(page 57)

Bullion stitch loop
(page 57)

Celtic knot stitch
(page 56)

Chain-stitch rose
(page 59)

Chinese knot stitch
(page 55)

Colonial knot stitch
(page 55)

Cross and twist stitch
(page 55)

English rose stitch
(page 57)

French knot stitch
(page 54)

French knot stitch
flowers (page 58)

Frilled petal or leaf stitch (page 56)

Four-legged knot stitch
(page 55)

Gwen's rose stitch
(page 58)

Jill's flower stitch
(page 59)

Knotted filler shapes
(page 58)

Knotted seed stitch
(page 58)

Raised buttonhole
stitch (page 56)

Raised spiderweb stitch
(page 59)

Spiderweb rose stitch
(page 59)

Spiderweb rose stitch
variation (page 59)

Tiny dragonfly stitch
(page 59)

Whip-stitch rose
(page 57)

Whip-stitch rose
variation (page 58)

Whip-stitch star
(page 56)

LAZY DAISY STITCHES (page 60)

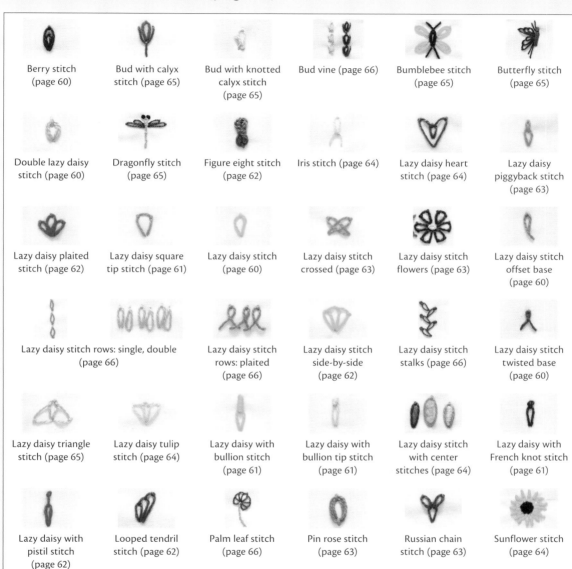

Berry stitch
(page 60)

Bud with calyx
stitch (page 65)

Bud with knotted
calyx stitch
(page 65)

Bud vine (page 66)

Bumblebee stitch
(page 65)

Butterfly stitch
(page 65)

Double lazy daisy
stitch (page 60)

Dragonfly stitch
(page 65)

Figure eight stitch
(page 62)

Iris stitch (page 64)

Lazy daisy heart
stitch (page 64)

Lazy daisy
piggyback stitch
(page 63)

Lazy daisy plaited
stitch (page 62)

Lazy daisy square
tip stitch (page 61)

Lazy daisy stitch
(page 60)

Lazy daisy stitch
crossed (page 63)

Lazy daisy stitch
flowers (page 63)

Lazy daisy stitch
offset base
(page 60)

Lazy daisy stitch rows: single, double
(page 66)

Lazy daisy stitch
rows: plaited
(page 66)

Lazy daisy stitch
side-by-side
(page 62)

Lazy daisy stitch
stalks (page 66)

Lazy daisy stitch
twisted base
(page 60)

Lazy daisy triangle
stitch (page 65)

Lazy daisy tulip
stitch (page 64)

Lazy daisy with
bullion stitch
(page 61)

Lazy daisy with
bullion tip stitch
(page 61)

Lazy daisy stitch
with center
stitches (page 64)

Lazy daisy with
French knot stitch
(page 61)

Lazy daisy with
pistil stitch
(page 62)

Looped tendril
stitch (page 62)

Palm leaf stitch
(page 66)

Pin rose stitch
(page 63)

Russian chain
stitch (page 63)

Sunflower stitch
(page 64)

CHAIN STITCHES (page 67)

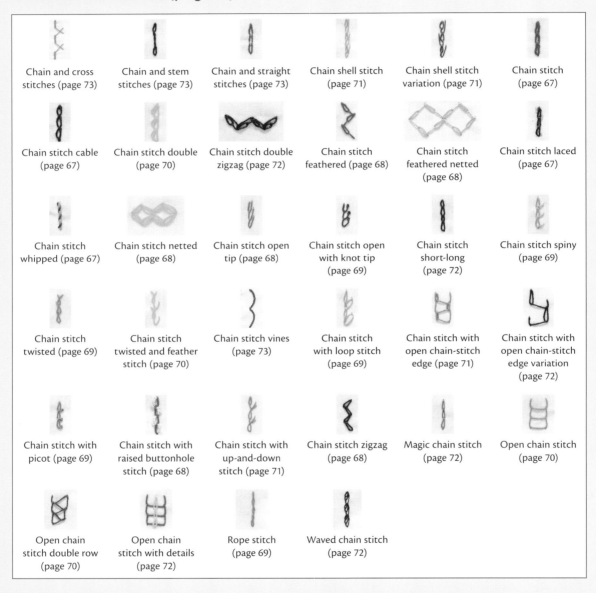

Chain and cross stitches (page 73)

Chain and stem stitches (page 73)

Chain and straight stitches (page 73)

Chain shell stitch (page 71)

Chain shell stitch variation (page 71)

Chain stitch (page 67)

Chain stitch cable (page 67)

Chain stitch double (page 70)

Chain stitch double zigzag (page 72)

Chain stitch feathered (page 68)

Chain stitch feathered netted (page 68)

Chain stitch laced (page 67)

Chain stitch whipped (page 67)

Chain stitch netted (page 68)

Chain stitch open tip (page 68)

Chain stitch open with knot tip (page 69)

Chain stitch short-long (page 72)

Chain stitch spiny (page 69)

Chain stitch twisted (page 69)

Chain stitch twisted and feather stitch (page 70)

Chain stitch vines (page 73)

Chain stitch with loop stitch (page 69)

Chain stitch with open chain-stitch edge (page 71)

Chain stitch with open chain-stitch edge variation (page 72)

Chain stitch with picot (page 69)

Chain stitch with raised buttonhole stitch (page 68)

Chain stitch with up-and-down stitch (page 71)

Chain stitch zigzag (page 68)

Magic chain stitch (page 72)

Open chain stitch (page 70)

Open chain stitch double row (page 70)

Open chain stitch with details (page 72)

Rope stitch (page 69)

Waved chain stitch (page 72)

BARB STITCHES (page 74)

Barb stitch (page 74)

Barb stitch angled (page 74)

Barb stitch capped (page 75)

Barb stitches crossed: barb stitch angled, barb stitch capped, barb stitch angled different lengths (page 77)

Barb stitches crossed: barb stitch with knot tip (page 77)

Barb stitch flowers (page 79)

Barb stitch grouped row (page 79)

Barb stitch looped (page 75)

Barb stitch looped crossed (page 77)

Barb stitch random netting (page 79)

Barb stitch stalks (page 79)

Barb stitch up and down (page 76)

Barb stitch with arrow tip detail (page 75)

Barb stitch with knot tip (page 74)

Barb stitch with picot stitch (page 75)

Barb stitch with twisted loop (page 75)

Barbed wire stitch (page 76)

Barbed wire stitch variation (page 76)

Boomerang stitch (page 75)

Crossed wire stitch (page 76)

Crossed wire stitch elongated (page 77)

Crossed wire stitch variation (page 77)

Dandelion stitch (page 78)

Fireworks stitch (page 78)

Little fly stitch (page 78)

Santa Fe star stitch (page 78)

Tiny butterfly stitch (page 78)

Wind stitch (page 78)

BLANKET AND BUTTONHOLE STITCHES (page 80)

Bell flower stitch (page 89)

Blanket and chain stitches (page 88)

Blanket and chain stitch variations (page 89)

Blanket and lazy daisy stitches (page 87)

Blanket and pistil stitches (page 87)

Blanket and pistil stitch variations (page 89)

Blanket and scroll stitches (page 88)

Blanket and stem stitches (page 88)

Blanket mock sheaf stitch (page 86)

Blanket stitch (page 80)

Blanket stitch angled (page 82)

Blanket stitch angled variations (page 84)

Blanket stitch closed (page 84)

Blanket stitch closed or crossed variations (page 85)

Blanket stitch closed shapes (page 90)

Blanket stitch closed with details (page 85)

Blanket stitch cobweb (page 91)

Blanket stitch crossed (page 84)

Blanket stitch feathered (page 89)

Blanket stitch flower (page 90)

Blanket stitch height and spacing variations (page 80)

Blanket stitch leaf (page 91)

Blanket stitch locked zipper (page 81)

Blanket stitch looped (page 82)

Blanket stitch looped/closed (page 87)

Blanket stitch looped/ closed shapes (page 90)

Blanket stitch looped zipper (page 83)

Blanket stitch mirrored (page 84)

Blanket stitch netted (page 89)

Blanket stitch stalk or row (page 88)

Blanket stitch up and down (page 81)

Blanket stitch with knot tip (page 85)

Blanket stitch with knot tip angled (page 86)

Blanket stitch with loose knot stitch (page 82)

Blanket stitch with picot stitch (page 86)

Blanket stitch with twisted loop (page 83)

Blanket stitch whipped or with buttonhole stitch (page 83)

Blanket stitch zipper (page 81)

Blanket stitches and chain stitch open tip (page 88)

Boxed star stitch (page 90)

Buttonhole circle stitch (page 90)

Crossed triangle stitch (page 91)

Leaves and stem stalk or row (page 88)

Looped petal row (page 87)

Magic blanket stitch (page 87)

Pretty butterfly stitch (page 91)

Shell stitch (page 86)

Shell stitch row (page 86)

Sunrise stitch (page 91)

Tree stitch (page 90)

FLY STITCHES (page 92)

 Agapanthus stitch (page 96)

 Crown stitch (page 98)

 Fern stitch modern (page 94)

 Fishhook stitch (page 98)

 Fly stitch (page 92)

 Fly stitch capped (page 97)

 Fly stitch chain link (page 98)

 Fly stitch double (page 97)

 Fly stitch fancy link (page 98)

 Fly stitch flowers (page 95)

 Fly stitch flower variations (page 95)

 Fly stitch long arm crossed group or row (page 97)

 Fly stitch long arm straight or angled (page 92)

 Fly stitch mirrored (page 96)

 Fly stitch mock chevron (page 98)

 Fly stitch netted (page 98)

 Fly stitch offset (page 92)

 Fly stitch plaited (page 98)

 Fly stitch reversed (page 97)

 Fly stitch side by side (page 95)

 Fly stitch soft edges (page 93)

 Fly stitch stacked and variations (page 97)

 Fly stitch straight edge grouped (page 93)

 Fly stitch twisted (page 94)

 Fly stitch up and down (page 95)

 Fly stitch variations (page 92)

 Fly stitch with bullion stitch tail (page 94)

 Fly stitch with chain-stitch edge (page 94)

 Fly stitch with French knot stitch (page 93)

 Fly stitch with lazy daisy stitch (page 94)

 Fly stitch with loose knot stitch (page 94)

 Fly stitch with pistil stitch (page 93)

 Fly stitch with straight edge (page 93)

 Fly stitch with straight-edge variations (page 93)

 Frilly spiderweb stitch (page 96)

Heart stitch (page 97)

Hourglass stitch (page 92)

Magic fly stitch (page 95)

Skeleton leaf stitch (page 96)

Triangle stitch (page 96)

Wisteria stitch (page 96)

FEATHER STITCHES (page 99)

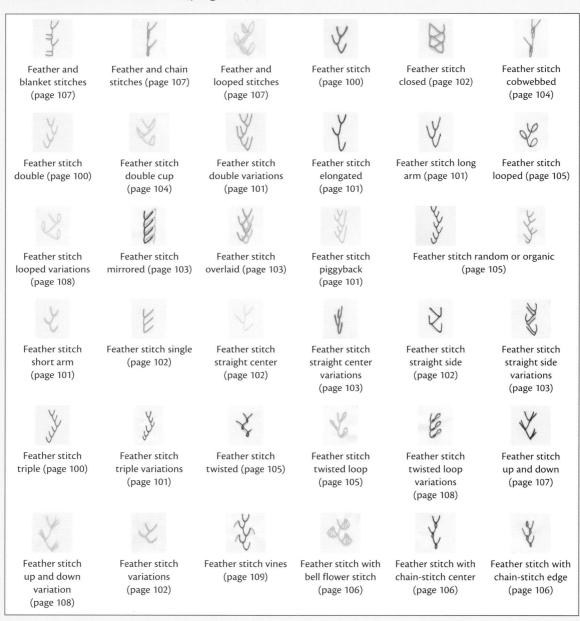

Feather and blanket stitches (page 107)

Feather and chain stitches (page 107)

Feather and looped stitches (page 107)

Feather stitch (page 100)

Feather stitch closed (page 102)

Feather stitch cobwebbed (page 104)

Feather stitch double (page 100)

Feather stitch double cup (page 104)

Feather stitch double variations (page 101)

Feather stitch elongated (page 101)

Feather stitch long arm (page 101)

Feather stitch looped (page 105)

Feather stitch looped variations (page 108)

Feather stitch mirrored (page 103)

Feather stitch overlaid (page 103)

Feather stitch piggyback (page 101)

Feather stitch random or organic (page 105)

Feather stitch short arm (page 101)

Feather stitch single (page 102)

Feather stitch straight center (page 102)

Feather stitch straight center variations (page 103)

Feather stitch straight side (page 102)

Feather stitch straight side variations (page 103)

Feather stitch triple (page 100)

Feather stitch triple variations (page 101)

Feather stitch twisted (page 105)

Feather stitch twisted loop (page 105)

Feather stitch twisted loop variations (page 108)

Feather stitch up and down (page 107)

Feather stitch up and down variation (page 108)

Feather stitch variations (page 102)

Feather stitch vines (page 109)

Feather stitch with bell flower stitch (page 106)

Feather stitch with chain-stitch center (page 106)

Feather stitch with chain-stitch edge (page 106)

FEATHER STITCHES: CONTINUED (page 99)

Feather stitch with chain-stitch edge or center variations (page 109)

Feather stitch with fly stitch detail (page 108)

Feather stitch with fly stitch detail variations (page 109)

Feather stitch with lazy daisy stitch detail (page 105)

Feather stitch with lazy daisy stitch detail variations (page 109)

Feather stitch with knot tip (page 106)

Feather stitch with loose knot stitch (page 107)

Feather stitch with outline stitches (page 107)

Feather stitch with sheaf stitch edge (page 108)

Fishnet stitch (page 104)

Magic feather stitch (page 100)

Maidenhair fern stitch (page 103)

Maidenhair fern stitch single (page 104)

FLEET STITCHES (page 110)

Fleet stitch (page 110)

Fleet stitch with arrow tip detail (page 110)

Fleet stitches crossed (page 111)

Fleet stitch flowers (page 112)

Fleet stitch long arm (page 110)

Fleet stitch looped (page 112)

Fleet stitch netted (page 113)

Fleet stitch offset (page 110)

Fleet stitch offset row plaited (page 113)

Fleet stitch plaited (page 113)

Fleet stitch reversed (page 111)

Fleet stitch row (page 111)

Fleet stitch twisted loop (page 112)

Fleet stitch up and down (page 112)

Fleet stitch twisted with French knot (page 112)

Fleet stitch with angled arm (page 110)

Fleet stitch with knot tip (page 111)

Fleet stitch with lazy daisy stitch (page 111)

Fleet stitch with loose knot stitch (page 111)

Fleet stitch with pistil stitch (page 111)

Snowflake stitch (page 112)

Steeple and cross stitch (page 110)

CRETAN STITCHES (page 114)

Cretan and blanket stitches (page 121)

Cretan and coral stitches (page 121)

Cretan and stem stitches (page 120)

Cretan stitch 3-row (page 115)

Cretan stitch 4-row (page 114)

Cretan stitch angled 3-row (page 115)

Cretan stitch angled 4-row (page 115)

Cretan stitch angled tips (page 117)

Cretan stitch capped (page 117)

Cretan stitch double-single (page 117)

Cretan stitch double tip (page 119)

Cretan stitch forked tip (page 120)

Cretan stitch laced (page 118)

Cretan stitch looped (page 116)

Cretan stitch looped and chain stitches (page 121)

Cretan stitch offset angle (page 118)

Cretan stitch short tip (page 116)

Cretan stitch spacing variation (page 115)

Cretan stitch sprig tip (page 120)

Cretan stitch straight/angled (page 117)

Cretan stitch tip variations (page 119)

Cretan stitch triple tip (page 119)

Cretan stitch up and down (page 118)

Cretan stitch with arrow tip detail (page 117)

Cretan stitch with chain stitch (page 119)

Cretan stitch with feather stitch (page 118)

Cretan stitch with knot tip (page 116)

Cretan stitch with loose knot (page 116)

Cretan stitch overlaid (page 121)

Steeple and cross stitch row (page 117)

CROSS STITCHES (page 122)

Chained cross stitch row (page 127)

Cross and fly stitch row (page 127)

Cross and fly stitch stars (page 126)

Cross and French knot stitches (page 123)

Cross and straight stitch shapes (page 125)

Crossed fly stitch long tail (page 124)

Crossed lazy daisy stitch (page 125)

Crossed lazy daisy stitch long arm (page 124)

Crossed pistil stitch (page 123)

Crossed star stitch (page 125)

Crossed wing stitch (page 126)

Crosshatch stitch (page 124)

Cross stitch (page 122)

Cross stitch capped (page 123)

Cross stitch doubled (page 125)

Cross stitch doubled and fly stitch shapes (page 126)

Cross stitch long arm (page 123)

Cross stitch row (page 122)

Cross stitch row capped (page 127)

Cross stitch row netted (page 127)

Cross stitch row overlaid (page 127)

Cross stitch row with stem stitches (page 127)

Cross stitch short cross (page 123)

Cross stitch short cross with arrow tip detail (page 123)

Cross stitch single-double (page 123)

Cross stitch with straight stitches (page 123)

Cross stitch twisted (page 124)

Cross stitch vertical (page 123)

Cross stitch vertical offset (page 123)

Cross stitch vertical shapes (page 125)

Cross stitch vertical with cross stitch details (page 125)

Four-corner cross stitch (page 126)

Four-corner cross stitch star (page 126)

Four-corner cross stitch with details (page 126)

Magic cross stitch (page 124)

Thorn stitch (page 127)

Woven cross stitch (page 124)

HERRINGBONE STITCHES (page 128)

Herringbone and
blanket stitches
(page 132)

Herringbone and chain
stitches (page 134)

Herringbone and coral
stitches (page 132)

Herringbone and cross
stitches (page 134)

Herringbone and cross
stitch single (page 133)

Herringbone and cross
stitch single variations
(page 133)

Herringbone and fly
stitches (page 134)

Herringbone and
fly stitch long tail
(page 134)

Herringbone and
French knot stitches
(page 134)

Herringbone–lazy
daisy long arm stitch
(page 131)

Herringbone and pistil
stitch (page 131)

Herringbone double
stitch (page 130)

Herringbone long arm
stitch (page 129)

Herringbone random
filling stitch (page 133)

Herringbone stitch
(page 128)

Herringbone stitch
boxed (page 129)

Herringbone stitch
capped (page 133)

Herringbone stitch
cascade (page 130)

Herringbone stitch
condensed (page 130)

Herringbone stitch
elongated (page 129)

Herringbone stitch
laced (page 132)

Herringbone stitch
netted (page 130)

Herringbone stitch
overlaid (page 132)

Herringbone stitch
short-long (page 129)

Herringbone stitch
twisted (page 130)

Herringbone stitch
with arrow tip detail
(page 133)

Herringbone stitch with
blanket stitch overlay
(page 134)

Herringbone stitch with
details (page 133)

Herringbone stitch with
lazy daisy stitch details
(page 134)

Herringbone stitch with
loose knot (page 131)

Herringbone with pistil
stitch details (page 134)

CAPPED STITCHES (page 135)

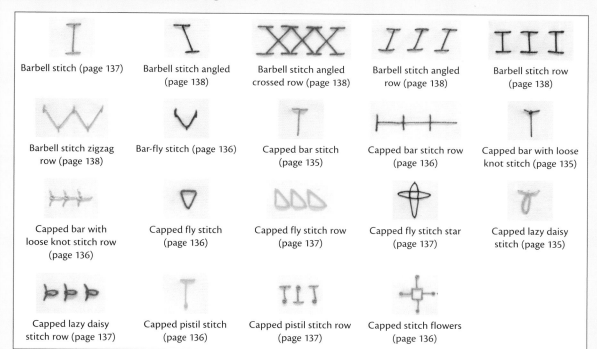

Barbell stitch (page 137)

Barbell stitch angled (page 138)

Barbell stitch angled crossed row (page 138)

Barbell stitch angled row (page 138)

Barbell stitch row (page 138)

Barbell stitch zigzag row (page 138)

Bar-fly stitch (page 136)

Capped bar stitch (page 135)

Capped bar stitch row (page 136)

Capped bar with loose knot stitch (page 135)

Capped bar with loose knot stitch row (page 136)

Capped fly stitch (page 136)

Capped fly stitch row (page 137)

Capped fly stitch star (page 137)

Capped lazy daisy stitch (page 135)

Capped lazy daisy stitch row (page 137)

Capped pistil stitch (page 136)

Capped pistil stitch row (page 137)

Capped stitch flowers (page 136)

CHEVRON STITCHES (page 139)

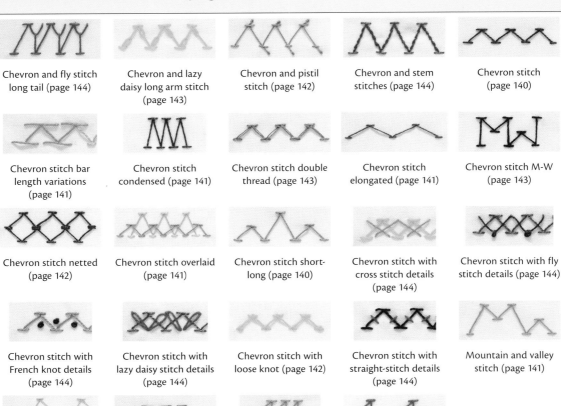

Chevron and fly stitch long tail (page 144)

Chevron and lazy daisy long arm stitch (page 143)

Chevron and pistil stitch (page 142)

Chevron and stem stitches (page 144)

Chevron stitch (page 140)

Chevron stitch bar length variations (page 141)

Chevron stitch condensed (page 141)

Chevron stitch double thread (page 143)

Chevron stitch elongated (page 141)

Chevron stitch M-W (page 143)

Chevron stitch netted (page 142)

Chevron stitch overlaid (page 141)

Chevron stitch short-long (page 140)

Chevron stitch with cross stitch details (page 144)

Chevron stitch with fly stitch details (page 144)

Chevron stitch with French knot details (page 144)

Chevron stitch with lazy daisy stitch details (page 144)

Chevron stitch with loose knot (page 142)

Chevron stitch with straight-stitch details (page 144)

Mountain and valley stitch (page 141)

Rolling hills stitch (page 140)

Sawtooth stitch (page 142)

Sawtooth stitch plaited (page 143)

Sawtooth stitch variation (page 143)

EMBELLISHMENT STITCHES (page 145)

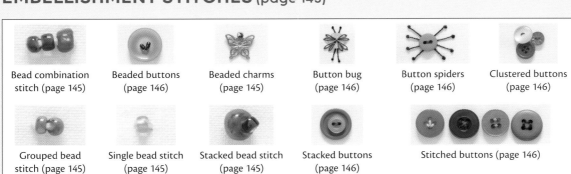

Bead combination stitch (page 145)

Beaded buttons (page 146)

Beaded charms (page 145)

Button bug (page 146)

Button spiders (page 146)

Clustered buttons (page 146)

Grouped bead stitch (page 145)

Single bead stitch (page 145)

Stacked bead stitch (page 145)

Stacked buttons (page 146)

Stitched buttons (page 146)

For the Love of Embroidery

Embroidered from the Heart

EARLY INFLUENCES

I dabble in all types of needlework, but embroidery remains to be my favorite form of expression. I learned to embroider at the age of seven, sitting at my mom's side happily stitching my designs—one hand holding a small wooden embroidery hoop and the other wielding a needle threaded with cotton floss. From that time forward, not a day has gone by without taking a stitch.

Many women influenced my love for embroidery; one was Erica Wilson. I remember my mom and I watching her TV program, and I thought,

Wow—I want to do this too! My mom owned several of her books, which now have been passed down to me.

In addition to those books, I have gathered a collection of treasured reference books from my favorite authors. Each author lends her own take on the stitches, with examples that reflect their style and expertise. I refer to these books when I am trying to expand my knowledge with new techniques, experimenting with ways that these stitches can be adapted to the type of embroidery I use.

Glamour Girl

Big Leaves

Getting Started

Our House is a Very, Very Fine House

Before you begin embroidery, you must first construct a fabric base. This will determine the overall design for your embroidery and embellishments. You could choose a solid color wholecloth base, a base with one or more printed fabrics, or a foundation strip- or crazy-pieced design. Additional design elements such as ribbons, trims, or laces offer more embroidery and embellishment opportunities.

MATERIALS

Choose fabrics that reflect the design and style of your project. Add components such as trims, embroidery threads, and embellishments to complement the composition. Work with colors that you like and ones that work within the color schemes of your home.

Fabrics

Choose good-quality fabrics with a high thread count that will hold up under extensive hand stitching and additional components.

Solid-color and printed cotton—as well as denim, linen, wool, and silk—are suitable for the base of your project. Specialty fabrics such as velvet, moiré, batiks and hand-dyed fabrics, and felt can add an interesting design element.

Tip When working with a print or batik, remember that some fabric will show through the embroidery stitches. Choose patterns that won't overpower the stitching.

Lace and Trims

- Use lace yardage and appliqués as part of a pieced design or as a shape to embroider around. Stitch them down by hand with sewing thread; then embroider on or around the edges.

- You can stitch grosgrain, jacquard, satin, and velvet ribbons to the base by hand or by machine. Embroider along the edges or through the middle of the ribbon.

- Use braids, cords, and trims to cover a raw edge or to create a design. Stitch braids and trims to the base by hand; then add embroidered stitches. Couch or embroider cords in place with embroidery threads.

Stabilizers

I recommend some form of stabilizer whether the base is pieced onto a muslin foundation, fused to a piece of interfacing, or backed with batting. The stabilizer minimizes wrinkling and distortion of the fabric and eliminates the need for an embroidery hoop.

1. Fabric

2. Trims

3. Appliqués

4. Felt

5. Stabilizers

EMBROIDERY THREADS

Embroidery threads come in a variety of materials, weights, and colors, in both twisted and flat threads. If your fabrics have a strong print, choose one type of thread in solid colors to add design details without competing with the fabric base. If your fabrics are a solid color or muted batik, use a variety of threads and colors to enhance and create a rich, interesting look.

Perle Cotton

Perle cotton is a 2-ply twisted cotton thread that comes on a ball or in a twisted skein in sizes #3, #5, #8, and #12 (the lower the number, the thicker the thread). It is worked as a single thread.

Floss

Stranded floss is a flat thread that comes in a skein of 6 strands. Embroidered designs are worked with 1 or more strands. Cotton and silk floss have a subtle color and texture; linen floss has a soft color but coarse texture; rayon floss and some silk flosses have a shiny, supple texture.

Specialty Colors

Ombré, variegated, and hand-dyed colorways can lend a unique touch to any design. When working with this thread, I try not to think out the colorway too seriously—I just cut the thread from the skein or ball and begin stitching.

Tip If it is imperative to have a similar colorway for balance, find the color repeat and then cut the thread into equal lengths.

Beading Threads

For bead embroidery, you will need special beading thread and needles. I recommend these threads:

- **Silamide size A:** A 2-ply waxed nylon thread on a card or spool
- **Nymo size B:** A flat, supple nylon thread on a small bobbin

1. Perle cotton #5, #8, and #12

2. Hand-dyed perle cotton

3. Stranded floss: cotton, silk, linen, and rayon

4. Beading threads

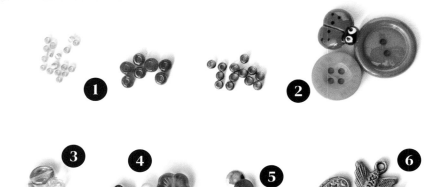

1. Seed beads

2. Buttons

3. Larger beads

4. Glass charms

5. Sequins

6. Metal charms

EMBELLISHMENTS

Little extras such as beads, buttons, charms, and sequins can give your project an identity that is unique to your own style while telling the story of the project. These embellishments come in a variety of materials, shapes, sizes, and colors. Added touches and unexpected details make the project that much more personal.

- Beads can be stitched to the base with beading thread, with perle cotton #12, or with 1 strand of floss as part of an embroidery stitch.

- Buttons can be stitched to the base with perle cotton and embroidered using a variety of threads and embroidery stitches.

- Sequins usually have a center hole and can be stitched in place using several of the bead embroidery stitches or with perle cotton #12.

- Charms have a hole placed in the design and can be stitched in place using several of the bead embroidery stitches or with perle cotton #12.

Heart Sampler

Embroidery Terminology

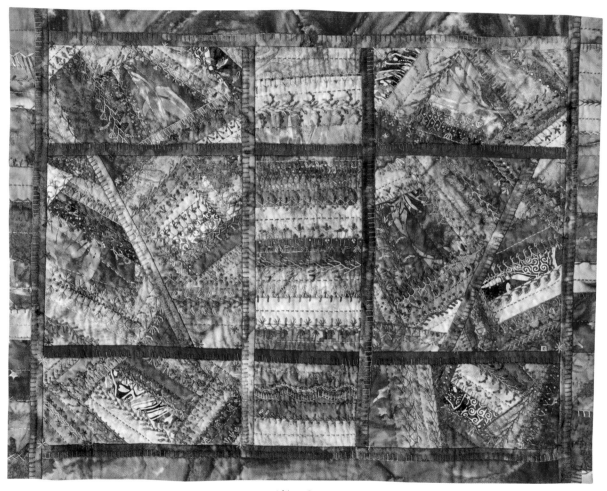

African Sunset

All of the embroidery stitches in this book are hand stitched onto a fabric base. These use a variety of materials and include traditional stitches, raised and textured stitches, and beaded stitches. They are considered free-form stitches because they are worked without the aid of a counted cloth or canvas, though some of these stitches can be adapted to counted-cloth designs.

PRELUDE TO A STITCH

The main goal of this book, and of my work, is to teach and pass on this wonderful needlecraft of free-form embroidery. I am always striving to find the best way to instruct, demonstrate, and describe these techniques. My goal is for you to be successful, to feel confident, and to enjoy this beautiful craft.

The stitch families in this book fall under two main categories: individual and continuous stitches. Within these stitch families you will find composite, compound, and hybrid stitches, which are combinations of one or more stitches that create a larger individual stitch, are a continuous row of stitches, or are used to fill in a space or shape.

To help you become familiar with these stitches, I have listed the individual stitch family first, followed by the continuous stitch family that uses the same or similar form. In order to understand these similarities, I suggest that you study and become familiar with both the written and the drawn instructions for these stitches.

WHAT IS IN A NAME?

I often wonder to myself, *How was a stitch named?* It is apparent that some are named after the country of origin, some relate to the shape of the stitch, and others are just a wonderful mystery.

The lazy daisy stitch, also known as the *detached chain stitch*, is an individual stitch that is the beginning form of the chain stitch, a continuous stitch. The fly stitch, an individual stitch, is the beginning form of the feather stitch, a continuous stitch. The cross stitch, an individual stitch, is similar in form to the herringbone stitch, a continuous stitch.

As I studied the similarities of these individual and continuous stitch families, I decided to create three additional individual stitch families. These individual stitches help to explain their similar continuous-stitch counterparts.

- The *barb stitch* is the beginning form of the blanket stitch.

- The *fleet stitch* is the beginning form of the cretan stitch.

- The *barbell stitch* is the beginning form of the chevron stitch.

With the exception of these new stitch families, I tried to keep any new stitch that I created simple in name, similar to the family name, or a description of the shape. I have listed most of the composite, compound, and hybrid stitches by the original stitch family names.

STITCH DEFINITIONS

Individual Stitches

Individual stitches are worked as a single unit or combined to create a larger unit. They are called *decorative* or *detail stitches* when added to a stitch as it is being formed or added to an existing stitch. They can be stitched onto or around previously worked stitches with the same thread or different threads.

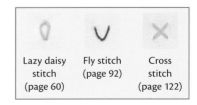

| Lazy daisy stitch (page 60) | Fly stitch (page 92) | Cross stitch (page 122) |

Continuous Stitches

Continuous stitches are created when the consecutive stitches are worked within or around the previous stitch. These can be worked as a border row of stitches on a straight or curved seam, imaginary line, or shape. Additional decorative and detail stitches can be added with the same thread or different threads.

Outline stitch (page 47)   Blanket stitch (page 80)   Chevron stitch (page 140)

Compound Stitches

Compound stitches are formed when an individual or detail stitch is added to an individual or continuous stitch in the process of forming the stitch. For an individual stitch, the second stitch completes the stitch. For a row of continuous stitches, the needle is brought back through the previous stitch to form the next stitch, and the pattern is then repeated.

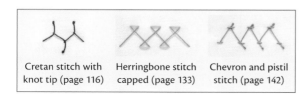

Cretan stitch with knot tip (page 116)   Herringbone stitch capped (page 133)   Chevron and pistil stitch (page 142)

Composite Stitches

Composite stitches are comprised of one or more individual or continuous stitches to create a flower, shape, or other form. These stitches can stand alone, be worked onto a border row of stitches, or be worked into a vignette. They can be worked with the same thread or different threads.

Wind stitch (page 78)   Heart stitch (page 97)   Woven cross stitch (page 124)

Hybrid Stitches

Hybrid stitches are created when a continuous stitch is combined with an individual or different continuous stitch. The second stitch can end the stitch or is ended and the row continues within the previous stitch. Or the second stitch is worked, and the pattern continues by repeating the first, then second, stitch.

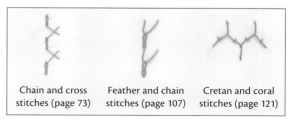

Chain and cross stitches (page 73)   Feather and chain stitches (page 107)   Cretan and coral stitches (page 121)

Grouped Stitches

Individual stitches can be worked into the previous stitch to create a plaited effect or to create a larger component or border row. Individual stitches can be repeated within a section to create a seeded effect, and both individual and continuous stitches can be repeated within a section to create a netted effect. Both individual and continuous stitches can be stitched with a second thread lacing through the first stitch, or a second row of stitches can be overlaid over the same stitch using a different color of thread.

Plaited Stitches

A plaited stitch is connected to the previous stitch by threading the needle under or over the thread of the previous stitch and then continuing to work the remaining steps of the stitch.

Seed Stitches and Filler Stitches

Seed stitching is used to fill in a shape or an entire area using a single stitch such as the straight stitch or French knot stitch. Filler stitches can be used on the tips of a previously worked stitch or to fill in an entire area.

Netted Stitches

Netted stitches start with a single stitch repeated and worked across a row or with a continuous row of stitches worked across a row. The following rows are then worked in the same color or a different color of thread, with the same stitch touching the tips of the previous row or catching the previous row of stitches.

Laced Details

Continuous stitches can be further enhanced with a second thread, ribbon, or yarn. This second thread comes through the fabric at the beginning of the stitch and is laced through the first row of stitches. When the row is finished, the thread goes down through the fabric after the last stitch.

Overlaid Stitches

Overlaid stitches can be an individual or continuous stitch that is worked in one color and thread. The same stitch or a different stitch is worked over the first stitch in a different color and/or thread.

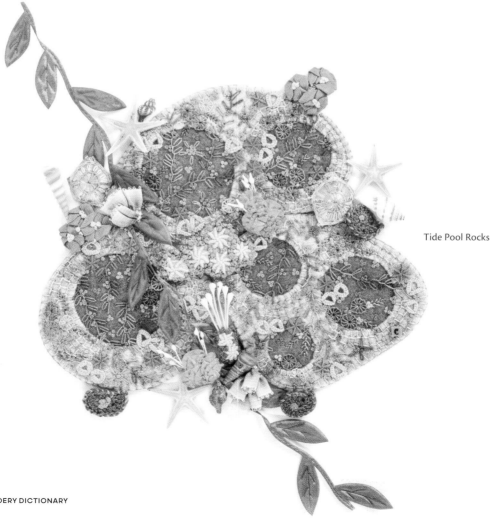

Tide Pool Rocks

Artfully Stitched

Darling Motif Sampler

Embroidery is such a wonderful form of self-expression. Your options are limitless, from the threads you choose to the stitches you embroider. Design inspirations can simply be a border row of stitches worked with decorative and detail stitches or a stitch worked around a shape, such as a template or found object.

ANATOMY OF A STITCH

If you know how a stitch is created, it will help you to understand, execute, and remember the stitch. As you learn the stitches, review the diagram of the stitch and the directions for the stitch, and then look for these key elements:

- Is the stitch worked straight in two motions, up and down?

- Is the stitch worked in three motions—come up and, in one motion, down and up with the thread looped under the needle?

- Is the stitch worked forward or backward?

- Is the stitch worked across the row or up and down the row?

- Is the stitch worked on a line, or above or below a line, or at an angle from a line?

The Form of a Stitch

In the directions for each new stitch, there will be a diagram of the basic points or steps that the needle will take. The positioning of these points forms the height and width of the stitch. You can alter the shape of the stitch by changing the positioning and distance between these points. These points can be varied to create different effects.

1. Stitch width is the distance between points **A** and **B**.
2. Stitch height is the distance between points **B** and **C**.

Points **A**, **B**, and **C** evenly spaced

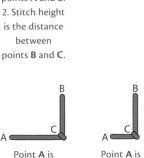

Point **A** is widened from points **B** and **C**.

Point **A** is shortened from points **B** and **C**.

The Style of a Stitch

An embroidery stitch can change in shape according to the design of the project, the type of threads used, and the style of the artist. Below is an example of the blanket stitch worked in three different sizes of thread and the feather stitch worked in several styles.

Blanket stitch worked in perle cotton #5, #8, and #12

Classic embroidery is where the stitches are worked evenly.

Classic

Contemporary embroidery is where the stitches are worked elongated or shortened with variations in spacing and size.

Contemporary

Organic embroidery is where the stitches are worked with a serendipitous approach, with no concern for accuracy or evenness in size and shape.

Organic

WORKING THE STITCHES

A question that I am often asked is, "Why don't my stitches look like yours?" More often than not, it is as simple as the way you are holding the fabric and the direction that you are working the stitch.

Work the border row stitches to the end of the row or pattern, and then knot and cut the thread. Work individual stitches alone or in groups, following the design or pattern, and then knot and cut the thread.

Stitch Direction

When working the stitches, keep in mind the direction of the stitch relative to the overall design. Is it relative to work a stitch up rather than down, or is a stitch worked into or away from the design?

For instance, the chain stitch can be worked in any direction from a design, but the tips of the feather stitch alter, depending on whether the stitch begins away from the design or vice versa.

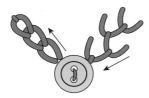

Chain stitch worked out of a vignette.
Feather stitch worked into a vignette.

Individual stitches can start at the center of the shape or can be worked toward the center of the shape.

Lazy daisy stitch
worked into a flower

Fly stitch worked
into a flower

Lines and Shapes

When working a row of stitches across a seam or line in a pattern, begin at one edge and work to the other edge. When working a continuous row of stitches around a shape or curve, begin at a point and work the stitches around the shape. When working a border row stitch, gauge the length of the stitches so that the last stitch can be worked into the first stitch.

First stitch

Last stitch

Chain stitch worked
in a line

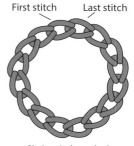

First stitch   Last stitch

Chain stitch worked
around a circle shape

Variations in Stitch Technique

When stitching around an appliqué shape, a button, a piece of trim, or through several layers of fabric, it is easier to perform the stitch like the chain or blanket stitch in three strokes—up, down, up—rather than in two strokes as the directions indicate.

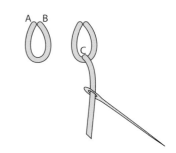

1. Come up at **A**.

2. Go down at **B**, pulling the thread slightly to form the stitch.

3. Come up at **C**, pulling the thread all the way through.

Adding Thread

CAUGHT STITCHES: FEATHER, BLANKET, CRETAN, OR CHAIN STITCH

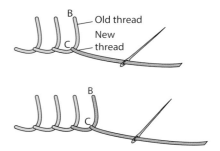

1. Stitch **B** of a looped stitch down through the fabric, but do not pull the thread taut. Stitch the new thread through the loop at **C**. Pull the old thread to form the loop.

2. Stitch 1 or 2 stitches with the new thread; then knot and cut the old thread. Continue to stitch with the new thread.

STRAIGHT STITCHES: OUTLINE, STEM, HERRINGBONE, OR CHEVRON

Knot and cut the old thread after **B**. Start the new thread at **C**.

Tip When you are adding lacing or whipped stitches to a previously worked stitch, begin with enough thread to complete the stitch.

CONSERVING THREAD

Embroider the design with minimal thread trails on the wrong side of the fabric. If the trail will be longer than ¾″ (1.9cm), knot and cut the thread; then restart the stitch in the next location. If somehow the threads on the wrong side get pulled wonky or out of shape, this will preserve the shape of the stitch.

THE PERFECT STITCH

Free-form embroidery is worked without the aid of a canvas or counted cloth, but that does not mean that you are not allowed to work with a drawn pattern.

Marking Pens

Air- or water-erasable marking pens can be used to mark a line or starting point for an embroidery stitch or design.

TEMPLATE AND PEN TIPS

- Test the marking pen or pencil first to make sure the line disappears or can be washed away.

- Hold the stencil steady with one hand; then mark the template with the other.

- Hold the pen or pencil upright in the channel when marking the design.

Rulers and Gauges

Rulers and seam gauges can be used to mark a line for embroidery or to mark off the distance between stitches or motifs. The lines can be drawn directly onto the fabric or onto temporary adhesive tapes.

Muslin with line marked off in ¼" (6.4mm) intervals, chain stitch

1. Choose a space or seam that you want to embroider over.

2. Place the ruler next to the line and draw the length of the line with a marking pen.

3. Embroider the stitch along the marked line.

Marked Tapes

Quilter¢s Tape is a ¼" (6.4mm) temporary adhesive tape that can be used for accurate spacing to create evenly stitched border rows. The spacing can be adjusted to the size and shape of the line or seam that you are working with.

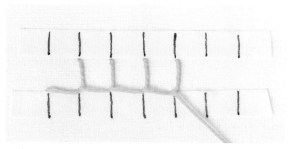

Quilter's Tape marked off in ¼" (6.4mm) intervals, blanket stitch

1. With a marking pen or pencil, draw a top and bottom line on the fabric for the measurement of the stitch width.

2. Place a piece of tape on each line.

3. With a permanent marker or pencil, mark off both pieces of tape at the same time in increments that will work for your design.

4. Embroider the stitch within the 2 marked lines.

Specialty Templates

Essential Collection Sampler

Diagram of template design

How to Mark a Template

1. Place the template onto the fabric.

2. With a marking pen or pencil, draw in the design.

3. Embroider the stitch along the marked line.

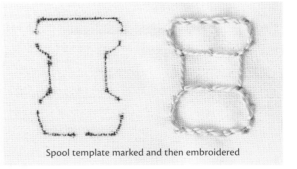

Spool template marked and then embroidered

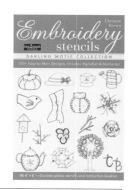

Specialty templates such as the fast2mark Embroidery Stencils, Essential Collection and the fast2mark Embroidery Stencils, Darling Motif Collection offer a variety of design choices. If you are using the stencils for the entire design, I suggest you make a diagram outlining where the templates will be placed.

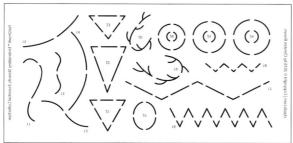

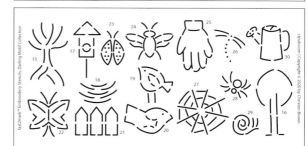

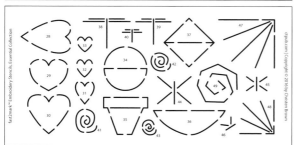

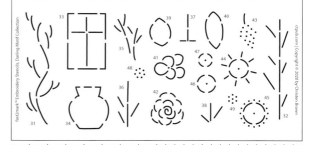

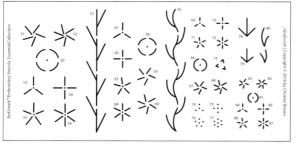

Artist Templates

Artist templates that have circular, square, or rectangular shapes can be used in a variety of ways. Depending on the size of the template, it can be used for an outline of a shape or used to define a shape. Follow the directions for How to Mark a Template (page 36).

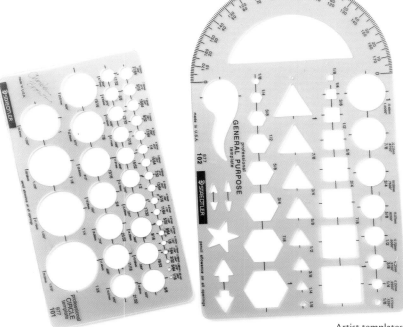

Artist templates

Found Objects

Found objects such as buttons, plastic thread spools, sewing machine bobbins, and manufacturing labels offer a variety of unique sizes and shapes that can be used for a template.

1. Place the object onto the fabric.

2. With a marking pen or pencil, draw around or through any holes of the object.

3. Embroider the stitch following the marked lines or points.

A sewing machine bobbin used for the points of a flower

Creating Your Own Templates

Embroidered heart-shaped layout

For a shape such as a heart, use copy paper and lightweight cardboard.

1. Cut out the paper shape with craft scissors.

2. Adhere the paper to a piece of lightweight cardboard with a glue stick.

3. Cut around the cardboard shape.

4. With a marking pen or pencil, draw around the shape.

5. Embroider the stitch along the marked line.

Custom Designs

You can customize a premade template design in order to fit your project by increasing or decreasing the size of the template with your printer.

INCREASING OR DECREASING SIZE

Actual size

Reduced 50%

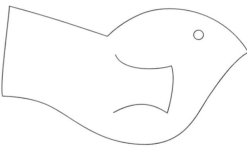

Increased 200%

1. Draw the template design onto a piece of copy paper.

2. Place the paper onto the scanner plate.

3. Program the printer to increase or decrease the size as desired.

4. Print the image.

TRANSFERRING THE TEMPLATE

Once the new template has been created, you can transfer it onto the fabric using the previous method (page 39) or one of the following methods: Wash-Away Stitch Stabilizer (by C&T Publishing) or a lightbox.

Wash-Away Stitch Stabilizer

This product is especially helpful if you are working with a dark or printed fabric.

Image transferred onto Wash-Away Stitch Stabilizer

1. Draw the template on a piece of copy paper.

2. Place the paper onto the scanner plate

3. Place a piece of the Wash-Away Stitch Stabilizer into the paper tray.

4. Print the image.

5. Cut close to the shape. Peel off the backing and then place onto the fabric base.

6. Embroider around the design.

7. Immerse the fabric in water to dissolve the paper template.

Using a Lightbox

1. Turn on the lightbox. Place the paper template on the surface of the box.

2. Place the fabric right side up on top of the paper template.

3. With a marking pen or pencil, draw around the design.

4. Embroider around the design.

Embroidery Stitch Dictionary

Psychedelic Balloons

Author's Note

If I could pass on one important thought, it would be that practice just makes sense. Perfection is not something that I strive for, but I myself feel more confident when I understand the stitches that I am working on.

I'm confident you will agree that allowing yourself the time to learn and experiment with a new technique will never be a waste of time. You are worth the time that it takes to prepare for your journey into embroidery. May that be a long enjoyable journey, and may your needles fly! –

INTRODUCTION

In this chapter, the embroidery stitches are presented as a family of stitches that can include one stitch and its variations or several similar stitches. All of these stitches can be worked in perle cotton and floss; heavier threads can be used for the laced, whipped, or braided details.

At the beginning of each stitch family, you will find generic information about the stitch, such as the type of stitch, how the stitch is formed, and how to use the stitch. You will also find suggestions for a temporary reference point, line, or grid that can be used in order to create a more accurate stitch.

The stitches fall under these categories: straight, looped, chained, or knotted. Each stitch is formed by varying the points of the stitch, which can be worked by separate stab motions, by stitching two points in a single motion, or a combination of both. The direction the stitch is worked can also vary. Some stitches are worked backward or forward, upward or downward, or some in a single position.

The samples of the stitches have been embroidered in the right-hand version. The basic stitch will include right-and left-handed illustrations of the stitch. The remaining stitches are illustrated in right-hand versions, though some stitches will include a note for the left-hand version.

The individual and continuous stitch families will include the basic stitches and show variations on length, width, spacing, and size. The additional stitches are composite, compound, and hybrid stitches, which are a combination of one or more stitches that create a larger individual stitch, a continuous row of stitches, or are used to fill in a space or shape. If the beginning of a stitch is related to another stitch, the directions will refer back to the first stitch.

For more information, please read the following chapters: Getting Started (page 23); Embroidery Terminology (page 27); Artfully Stitched (page 31); Design Workshop (page 147); and Tools, Tips and Tricks (page 153). *Note:* The stitches are listed under their respective sections in the Visual Guide (page 6).

STRAIGHT STITCHES

General Information

These individual stitches can be used as a single stitch, combined to create a border row, or added to another stitch to create a larger component.

The following stitches are formed by coming up at point **A** and going down at point **B** to create a straight line. If the stitch has a detail, it would continue with point **C** and **D** stitches or more.

For a reference guide, you could use an erasable pen to draw a line or 2 points the length of the stitch.

Straight Stitch

Come up at **A** and go down at **B**. This stitch can be worked vertically or horizontally.

Straight Stitch Couched

Come up at **A** and go down at **B**. Come up at **C** and go down at **D**. This stitch can be worked vertically or horizontally.

Straight Stitch Double

Work 2 straight stitches (at left) side by side in any direction.

Straight Stitch Double with Details

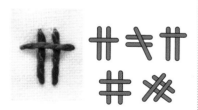

1. Work 2 straight stitches (above) side by side.

2. Work a third or fourth stitch across the first set of stitches to catch the first set of stitches.

Variations: *Change the length of the stitches, the number of catch stitches, or the position of the catch stitch.*

Straight Stitch Wrapped

LEFT-HANDED

RIGHT-HANDED

1. Work 1 straight stitch (above left).

2. Come up at **C**; slip the needle under and then over the first stitch, then through the loop of the second stitch. Go down at **D**.

Stamen Stitch

LEFT-HANDED   RIGHT-HANDED

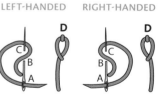

1. Come up at **A**. In one motion, go down at **B** and up at **C**; wrap the working thread over the needle and under the tip.

2. Pull the needle through the fabric. To finish the stitch, go down at **D**.

Pistil Stitch

LEFT-HANDED

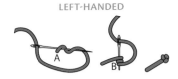

RIGHT-HANDED

1. Come up at **A**. Holding the needle a short distance away and close to the fabric, wrap the thread 1–3 times over the needle.

2. Go down at **B**. Pull the thread tight around the needle and pull the needle through the fabric.

Cattail Stitch

LEFT-HANDED

RIGHT-HANDED

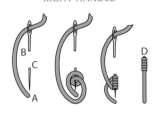

1. Come up at **A**. Working back toward **A**, in one motion go down at **B** and up at **C**, but do not pull the needle through the fabric.

2. Measure the distance between **B** and **C**; wrap the thread over the needle to equal that distance. Hold onto the needle and wraps as you gently pull the needle toward you through the fabric and wraps.

3. Pull the thread away from you, keeping the wraps even. To end the stitch, go down at **D**.

Arrow Tip Stitch

1. Work 1 straight stitch (page 43).

2. Work 1 straight stitch on either side of the first stitch, from **C** to **D**.

Swedish Split Stitch

Thread the needle with 2 colors of the same thread. Knot the tails together.

1. Work 1 straight stitch (page 43).

2. Come up at **C** between the 2 threads, go down at **D**, and catch one side of the stitch.

Sheaf Stitch

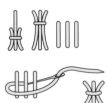

1. Work 3 evenly spaced straight stitches (page 43).

2. Come up under the middle of the center stitch, loop the thread around the stitches, and go down under the center.

3. Pull the loop taught, forming a catch stitch.

Variations: *Change the length of the stitches, the number of catch stitches, or the position of the catch stitch.*

Left-handed version: *In Step 2, loop the thread around the stitches from right to left.*

Ermine Stitch

1. Work 1 straight stitch (page 43).

2. Work 2 straight stitches, crossing over the first from **C** to **D** and **E** to **F**.

Variations: *Change the length of the stitches.*

Wheat Ear Stitch Modified

1. Work 2 straight stitches (page 43) from **A** to **B** and **C** to **D**.

2. Come up at **E**, pass the needle under the straight stitches, and go down at **F**.

Left-handed version: *In Step 2, reverse **E** for **F** and vice versa.*

Double-Crossed Corner Stitch

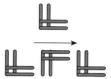

1. Work 1 vertical straight stitch double (page 43).

2. Work 1 horizontal straight stitch double.

Variations: *Change the length of the stitches or substitute a different stitch. Repeat the stitch in opposite directions to create a row.*

Five-Point Star Stitch

Draw in 5 points. Work 5 straight stitches (page 43) in this order: **A** to **B**, **C** to **D**, **E** to **F**, **G** to **H**, to **J**. Interlace the stitches where they cross over each other.

Variations: *Change the length of the stitches.*

Backstitch Shapes

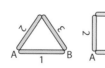

A. Triangle, **B.** Square

Triangle: Work 3 straight stitches (page 43) from **A** to **B** in the order shown.

Square: Work 4 straight stitches from **A** to **B** in the order shown.

Variations: *Change the length of the stitches or substitute a different stitch.*

Straight-Stitch Flowers

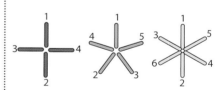

Choose a template and draw in the lines.

Work the straight stitches (page 43) in the order they are shown, from the outer tip to the center.

Variations: *Change the length of the stitches or substitute a different stitch.*

Optional: *Work a French knot (page 54) in the center of the flower.*

Straight-Stitch Stalks and Fillers

Straight stitch
(page 43)

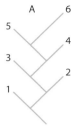 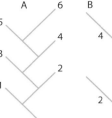 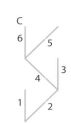

Stalk A   Stalk B   Stalk C

1. Choose one of the templates and draw in the shape.

2. Work the stitches in the order they are shown.

Variations: *Change the length of the stitches or substitute a different stitch.*

Pistil stitch, cattail stitch, arrow tip stitch

Filler shapes

Straight Stitch Grouped Row

Stamen stitch (page 43)

Arrow tip stitch (page 44)

Pistil stitch (page 44)

Work the stitches across a seam or line.

Variations: *Change the length of the stitches or substitute a different stitch.*

Mock Cretan Stitch

1. Work 1 straight stitch double at an angle (page 43).

2. Come up in the middle of the last stitch from the previous group. Work 1 straight stitch double.

3. Repeat Steps 1 and 2 to finish the row.

Variations: *Change the length of the stitches or substitute a different stitch.*

Left-handed version: *Work the stitches from right to left.*

Seed Stitch

Stitch 1 straight stitch double (page 43) close together. Repeat, randomly filling in the section or space.

Variations: *Change the length of the stitches or substitute a different stitch.*

Dot Stitch

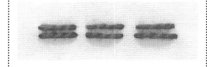

Work 1 row of straight stitch double (page 43) horizontally, vertically, or at an angle.

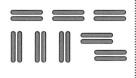

Dot Stitch Laced

1. Stitch 1 row of straight stitch double (page 43).

2. With a different color of thread, come up next to the stitch at the beginning of the row. Thread the needle under each of the stitches (not through the fabric).

3. To end the row, go down next to the last stitch in the row.

OUTLINE STITCHES

General Information

These continuous stitches can be used for a border row or to create a shape. After the stitch is formed, individual stitches can be added to the tips or around the base to create a larger design.

The following stitches are formed by coming up at point **A** and then, in one motion, going down at point **B** and up at point **C**, which then becomes point **A** for the following stitch. The stitch is worked continuously and would end at point **D**. If the stitch has a detail, it would continue with point **E** and **F** stitches or more.

For a reference guide and even spacing, you could draw a line with an erasable pen and mark off the line at even intervals.

Outline Stitch

LEFT-HANDED

RIGHT-HANDED

1. Come up at **A**, with the thread above the line. *Backstitch the needle in one motion down at **B** and up at **C**. Pull the needle through the fabric.

2. Repeat from * to finish the row, with **C** of the next stitch next to **B** of the previous stitch. To end the stitch, go down at **D**.

Stem Stitch

1. Come up at **A**, with the thread below the line. *Backstitch the needle in one motion down at **B** and up at **C**. Pull the needle through the fabric.

2. Repeat from * to finish the row, with **C** of the next stitch next to **B** of the previous stitch. To end the stitch, go down at **B**.

LEFT-HANDED

RIGHT-HANDED

Stem Stitch with Knot Tip

1. Come up at **A**, with the thread below the line. *Loop the thread over your finger and place the loop next to the fabric. Backstitch the needle in one motion down at an angle at **B**, through the loop, and up at **C**. Pull the thread tightly; then pull the needle through the fabric.

2. Repeat from * to finish the row, leaving a short distance between stitches. To end the stitch, go down at **D**.

LEFT-HANDED

RIGHT-HANDED

Linked Bullion Stitch

1. Come up at **A**. Follow Step 1 of the stem stitch (page 47) from *, but do not pull the thread through the fabric.

2. Measure the distance between **A** and **B**; wrap the thread around the needle to equal the distance. Hold onto the needle and wraps as you gently pull the needle away from you through the fabric and wraps. Pull the thread back toward the line, keeping the wraps even.

3. Repeat from * to finish the row. To end the stitch, go down at **D**.

LEFT-HANDED

RIGHT-HANDED

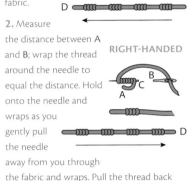

Stem Stitch Looped

1. Come up at **A**, with the thread below the line. *Backstitch the needle in one motion down at an angle at **B** and up at **C**. Wrap the working thread under the eye and the tip of the needle.

2. Place your thumb over the loop and pull the needle through the fabric. Go down at **D**. Come up at **E**.

3. Repeat from * to finish the row. To end the stitch, go down at **F**.

LEFT-HANDED

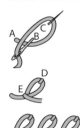

RIGHT-HANDED

Stem Stitch with Loose Knot

1. Work 1 stem stitch (page 47). Thread the needle under the stitch, and wrap the working thread under the tip of the needle. Pull the thread gently to form a loose knot.

2. Repeat Step 1 to finish the row. To end the stitch, go down at **B**.

LEFT-HANDED

RIGHT-HANDED

Backstitch

1. Come up at **A**. *Backstitch the needle in one motion, down at **B** and up at **C**. Pull the needle through the fabric. **C** now becomes **A**.

2. Repeat from * to finish the row. To end the stitch, go down at **B** of the last stitch.

LEFT-HANDED

RIGHT-HANDED

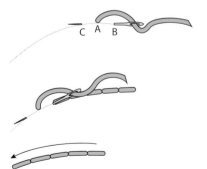

Backstitch Row Variations

Backstitch triangle

Backstitch zigzag

Backstitch serpentine

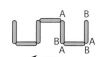

Follow the directions for the backstitch (page 48), using the suggestions below.

- **Triangle:** Work a pattern between 2 lines: 1 angled stitch, 1 straight stitch.

- **Zigzag:** Work the stitches at an angle between 2 lines.

  Note: *Vine B (page 51) can be used for accurate spacing.*

- **Serpentine:** Work a pattern between 2 lines: 1 vertical stitch, 1 horizontal stitch.

Left-handed version: *Work the stitches from left to right.*

Backstitch with Raised Buttonhole Stitch

1. Stitch 1 row of short backstitches (page 48). With the same thread or a different color of thread, come up at **A**, under the end of the stitch.

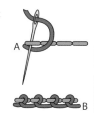

2. Follow Steps 2 and 3 for the raised buttonhole stitch (page 56), working 1 stitch into each backstitch. To end the stitch, go down at **B**.

Left-handed version: *Work the raised buttonhole stitches on the opposite end of the stitch.*

Running Stitch

1. Come up at **A**. *In one motion, go down at **B** and up at **C**. Pull the needle through the fabric. **C** now becomes **A**.

2. Repeat from * to finish the row. To end the stitch, go down at **B** of the last stitch.

Left-handed version: *Work the stitches from left to right.*

Running Stitch Variations

Running stitch laced

Running stitch whipped

Running stitch braided

1. Stitch 1 row of running stitches (at left).

2. With a different color or type of thread, come up next to the first stitch in the row. Follow the directions below for each stitch. To end the stitch, go down next to the last stitch in the row.

- **Laced:** Slide the needle under each stitch, working above or below them, creating a short loop between stitches.

- **Whipped:** Slide the needle under the stitch then over the stitch. Repeat for each stitch.

- **Braided:** Follow the directions for Laced (above), working in one direction and then in the opposite direction.

Split Stitch

Thread the needle with a heavier thread such as perle cotton #3 or #5.

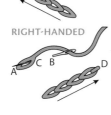

1. Come up at **A**. *Backstitch the needle in one motion down at **B** and up at **C** piercing the working thread. Pull the needle through the fabric.

2. Repeat from * to finish the row. To end the stitch, go down at **D**.

Magic Split Stitch

1. Thread the needle with 2 colors of thread. Come up at **A**. *Backstitch the needle in one motion down at **B** and up at **C**, with the threads on either side of the needle. Pull the thread through the fabric.

2. Repeat from * to the finish the row. To end the stitch, go down at **B**.

Pekinese Stitch

1. Stitch 1 row of medium-size backstitches (page 48). With a different color and heavier type of thread, come up at **A**.

2. *Slide the needle under the second stitch and then back under the first stitch, with the thread wrapped under the needle. Pull the thread through the stitches, leaving a gentle loop.

3. Repeat from * to finish the row, working 1 stitch ahead. To end the stitch, go down at **B**.

Coral Stitch

1. Come up at **A**, hold the working thread straight. *In one motion, go down at **B** and up at **C** slightly angled. Wrap the working thread under the tip of the needle.

2. Pull the needle through the fabric to form a knot.

3. Repeat from * to finish the row. To end the stitch, go down at **D** a slight distance away from the last knot.

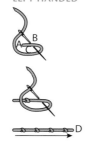

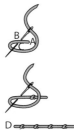

Coral Stitch Zigzag

Follow the directions for the coral stitch (at left), working the stitches at an angle between 2 lines.

Note: *Vine B (page 51) can be used for accurate spacing.*

Coral Stitch Double

1. Follow Step 1 of the coral stitch (at left). Repeat from * a short distance away to make a second knot.

2. Continue to make 2 coral stitches close together to finish the row. To end the stitch, go down at **D** a slight distance away from the last knot.

Stem/Outline Fern Stitch

Work 1 stem stitch (page 47) and then 1 outline stitch (page 47), working points **B** and **C** in both stitches at an angle. Alternate the stitches along the row.

Left-handed version:
Work the stitches from right to left.

Cable Stitch

Work 1 outline stitch (page 47) and then 1 stem stitch (page 47). Alternate the stitches along the row.

Left-handed version:
Work the stitches from right to left.

Couched Stitch

1. Stitch a length of thread onto the fabric; knot and cut the end.

2. With a different color or type of thread, come up next to one end of the thread. Work straight stitches (page 43) across the row.

Note: *A heavier thread such as perle cotton #3 or #5 can be used in Step 1, and a finer thread such as perle cotton #8 or #12 in Step 2.*

Spiderwebs: Corner and Round

Corner

Round

- **Spokes:** Work each straight stitch (page 43) in the order listed.
- **Web:** Begin at the outer edge and work long outline (page 47) or stem stitches (page 47) across the spokes, in rows or in a continuous stitch, back into the center of the web.

Vines with Templates

Vine A worked in the stem stitch (page 47)

Vine A

Vine B

Choose a template and draw the shape. Embroider with the stitch of your choice.

String of Pearls Stitch

1. Come up at **A**, holding the working thread straight. *Work a short perpendicular stitch, in one motion down at **B** and up at **C**. Wrap the working thread under the tip of the needle.

LEFT-HANDED

2. Pull the needle through the fabric to form a knot. Thread the needle under the bar and toward **A**. Lay the thread in a small circle around the knot.

3. Work a short stitch; in one motion go down at **D** and up at **E**. Wrap the working thread under the tip of the needle. Pull the needle through the fabric. **E** now becomes **A**.

RIGHT-HANDED

4. Repeat from * to finish the row. To end the stitch, go down at **F**.

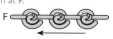

OUTLINE STITCHES

Portuguese Knotted Stem Stitch

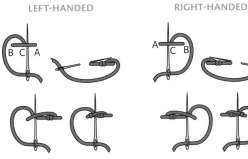

1. Come up at **A**. In one motion, go down at **B** and up at **C**. Pass the needle under the stitch, and wrap the thread around the stitch. Repeat for a second wrap.

2. In one motion, go down at **B** and up at **C**. Pass the needle under the stitch, and wrap the thread around the stitch. Pass the needle under the previous stitch and the new stitch.

3. Repeat Step 2 to finish the row. To end the stitch, go down at **D**.

Petal Stitch

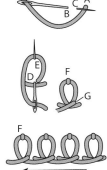

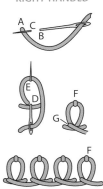

1. Work 1 stem stitch (page 47). *In one motion, go down at **D** and up at **E**. Wrap the working thread under the tip of the needle. Pull the needle through the fabric.

2. Go down at **F**. Come up at **G**, which now becomes **A** of the next stitch.

3. Repeat Steps 1 and 2 to finish the row. To end the stitch, go down at **F**.

Petal Stitch Variation

1. Follow Steps 1 and 2 for the petal stitch (above).

2. Work 1 outline stitch (page 47). Follow Step 1 of the petal stitch from *.

3. Repeat Steps 1 and 2 to finish the row. To end the stitch, go down at **F**.

Palestrina Knot Stitch

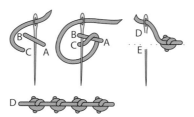

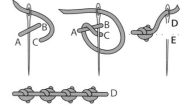

1. Come up at **A**. In one motion, go down at **B** and up at **C**.

2. *Wrap the thread over and under the stitch toward **A**. Wrap the thread a second time under the stitch toward **B**, wrapping the thread under the tip of the needle. Pull the thread gently around the stitch to form a knot.

3. In one motion, go down at **D** and up at **E**. **A** is now the end of the previous knot, **D** now becomes **B**, and **E** now becomes **C**.

4. Repeat from * to finish the row. To end the stitch, go down at **D**.

Bead Strand Stitch: Single and Double

Single

Double

LEFT-HANDED

RIGHT-HANDED

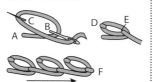

1. Come up at **A**, with the thread below the line. *In one motion, go down at **B** and up at **C**. Wrap the working thread under the eye and the tip of the needle.

2. Place your thumb over the loop and pull the needle through the fabric. Go down at **D**. Come up at **E**.

3. Repeat from * to finish the row. To end the stitch, go down at **F**.

Note: *For a single stitch, work the stitches on one side of the line. For a double stitch, work the stitches alternating on either side of the line.*

Snail Trail Stitch

1. Come up at **A**. *In one motion, go down at **B** and up at **C**.

2. Wrap the working thread over the needle and under the tip. Place your thumb over the loop and pull the needle through the fabric.

3. Repeat from * to finish the row a short distance away from the previous stitch. To end the stitch, go down at **D**.

LEFT-HANDED

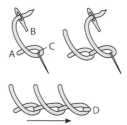

RIGHT-HANDED

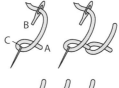

Scroll Stitch

1. Come up at **A**, with the thread above the line. *In one motion, go down at **B** and up at **C**.

2. Wrap the working thread under the eye and the tip of the needle. Place your thumb over the loop and pull the needle through the fabric to form a knot.

3. Repeat from * to finish the row a short distance away from the previous stitch. To end the stitch, go down at **D**.

LEFT-HANDED

RIGHT-HANDED

KNOTTED, WOVEN, AND WHIPPED STITCHES

General Information

These individual stitches can be used as a single stitch, combined to create a border row, or added to another stitch to create a larger component.

Each of the following unique stitches are worked with the thread wrapped around the needle to form a knot. In some, the needle is stitched into the fabric first and then wrapped with the thread. In others, a base is formed and then the needle is woven or whipped around that base.

For a reference guide, draw the beginning point or shape with an erasable pen.

CIRCLE SIZE AND THREAD CHOICE

See Blending Threads (page 156) for more information.

1″ (2.54cm) circle

- **Spokes:** Use perle cotton #5 thread.

- **Petals:** Use 3 strands of perle cotton #8 or 6 strands of floss.

¾″ (1.9cm) circle

- **Spokes:** Use perle cotton #8.

- **Petals:** Use 2 strands of perle cotton #12 or 4 strands of floss.

½″ (1.3cm) circle

- **Spokes:** Use perle cotton #12.

- **Petals:** Use 1 strand of perle cotton #12 or 2 strands of floss.

Color Choices

Solid color: Use the same size and color thread for the spokes and the petals.

Color blend: Choose 2 or more colors of the same size of thread for the petals.

Note: *Always start a whipped, woven, or wrapped stitch with a fresh length of thread long enough to complete the stitch.*

French Knot Stitch

1. Come up at **A**. Holding the needle close to the fabric, wrap the thread around the needle 1–5 times.

2. Pull the thread tight; hold the end of the tail of thread with your thumb. Go down at **B**. Pull the needle and thread through the fabric.

LEFT-HANDED

RIGHT-HANDED

Chinese Knot Stitch

LEFT-HANDED

1. Come up at A.

2. Loop the thread over your finger, and place the loop next to the fabric.

RIGHT-HANDED

3. Insert the needle inside the loop and into the fabric, but not all the way through. Pull the thread tightly; then pull the needle through the fabric.

Colonial Knot Stitch

LEFT-HANDED

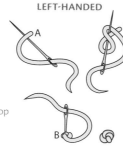

1. Come up at A. Thread the needle under the loop close to A.

2. Wrap the working thread under the eye and the tip of the needle. Tighten the thread firmly.

RIGHT-HANDED

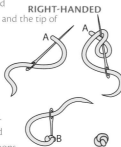

3. Insert the needle into the fabric at B. Pull the thread through the loops.

Bullion Stitch

LEFT-HANDED

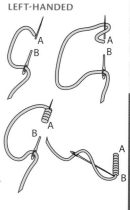

1. Come up at A. In one motion, go down at B and up next to A, but do not pull the thread through the fabric.

2. Measure the distance between A and B; *wrap the thread over the needle to equal the distance. Hold onto the needle and wraps as you gently pull the needle away from you and through the fabric and wraps.

RIGHT-HANDED

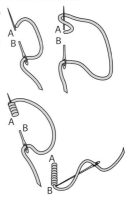

3. Pull the thread back toward you, keeping the wraps evenly spaced. To end the stitch, go down next to B.

Four-Legged Knot Stitch

LEFT-HANDED

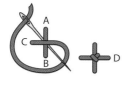

1. Work a straight stitch (page 43) from A to B. Come up at C. Pass the needle under the straight stitch. Wrap the working thread under the tip of the needle; pull the needle to form the knot.

RIGHT-HANDED

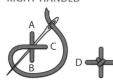

2. To end the stitch, go down at D.

Cross and Twist Stitch

LEFT-HANDED

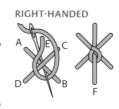

1. Work 1 straight stitch (page 43) from A to B; work a second stitch from C to D, crossing over the first stitch.

RIGHT-HANDED

2. Come up at E. Pass the needle under the thread at E and the crossed portion of the stitch. Wrap the working thread under the tip of the needle; pull the needle to form the knot.

3. To end the stitch, go down at F.

Whip-Stitch Star

LEFT-HANDED

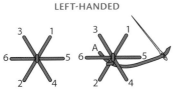

RIGHT-HANDED

1. Work 3 straight stitches (page 43). Stitch a short stitch across the center of the stitches.

2. Come up at **A**. Go under spokes 6 and 2. Whip the thread over spoke 2, then under spokes 2 and 4. Pull the thread close to the center.

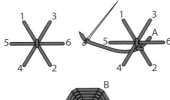

3. Continue whipping the thread over a spoke and then under the same spoke and the next spoke. To end the stitch, go down at **B** after the last spoke is covered.

Celtic Knot Stitch

LEFT-HANDED

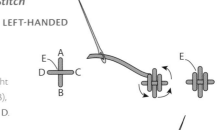

1. Work 2 straight stitches (page 43), **A** to **B** and **C** to **D**. Come up at **E**.

2. Work the thread over the bar at **D**, under the bar at **B**, over the bar at **C**, and under the bar at **A**.

RIGHT-HANDED

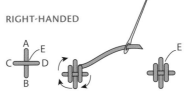

3. To end the stitch, go down at **E**.

Raised Buttonhole Stitch

LEFT-HANDED

Note: *The raised buttonhole stitch is worked off the base of an embroidered stitch and does not go through the fabric, other than at the beginning and end of the stitch.*

1. Work 1 straight stitch (page 43) for the base.

RIGHT-HANDED

2. Come up at **A**. *Pass the needle under the base stitch, and wrap the working thread under the tip of the needle. Pull the thread firmly around the base stitch.

3. Repeat from * to cover the base with stitches. To finish, go down at **B**.

Frilled Petal or Leaf Stitch

Frilled petal stitch   Frilled leaf stitch

1. Work 1 fly stitch (page 92) for the petal, or 1 lazy daisy stitch (page 60) for the leaf. Do not cut the thread.

2. Come up at **A**, close to the tip of the stitch. Follow Steps 2 and 3 for the raised buttonhole stitch (at left).

Left-handed version: *Work the raised buttonhole stitches on the opposite side of the beginning base stitch.*

English Rose Stitch

Center: Work a 3-wrap French knot (page 54) in the middle of the flower.

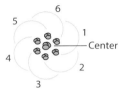

Work 6 French knots, 2 wraps each, around the center stitch.

Petals: Work the stitch from tip to center, following the directions for bullion stitch (page 55), with 15–18 wraps for each petal.

Left-handed version: Work petals counter-clockwise from center to tip.

Bullion Stitch Daisy

1. Draw the lines for the petals.

2. Follow the directions for the bullion stitch loop (above right). Work 1 petal for each line.

Optional: *Work a French knot stitch (page 54) in the center of the flower.*

Bullion Stitch Flower

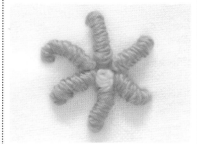

Petals: Follow the directions for English rose stitch petals (at left). Work the stitches in the order shown.

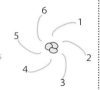

Center: Work a 3-wrap French knot (page 54) in the middle of the flower.

Bullion Stitch Loop

1. Follow Step 1 for the bullion stitch (page 55), with points **A** and **B** close together.

2. Wrap the thread clockwise over the needle 15 times. Go down at **C**; hold the wraps as you gently pull the thread through the fabric.

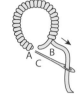

Whip-Stitch Rose

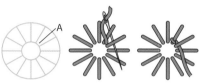

See Circle Size and Thread Choice (page 54).

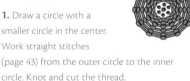

1. Draw a circle with a smaller circle in the center. Work straight stitches (page 43) from the outer circle to the inner circle. Knot and cut the thread.

2. Thread a chenille needle with 30″ (76.2 cm) of your thread choice. Come up at **A**. *Note: If you are working with 2 or more threads, twirl the needle to the right to twist the threads.*

3. Working clockwise, thread the needle over the spoke, and backstitch under the next 2 spokes. Gently pull the thread(s) to whip around the spoke.

4. Repeat Step 3, working around the spokes to the outer edges. To end, wrap the thread(s) over the previous spoke, and go down at **B**.

5. Fill the center with French knot stitches (page 54).

Notes: *In Step 1, the smaller the outer circle, the fewer spokes needed; a blanket stitch flower (page 90) can be substituted for the straight stitches. In Step 3, as you work around the outer spokes, you may have to work 1 spoke at a time.*

Left-handed version: *In Step 2, twirl the needle to the left to twist the thread(s). In Step 3, work the stitches counterclockwise.*

Whip-Stitch Rose Variation

Follow the directions for the whip-stitch rose (page 57), working with a color blend of threads for the petals.

Gwen's Rose Stitch

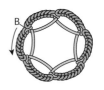

1. Draw a circle. Work 6 chain stitches (page 67) around the circle. Come up at **A**.

2. Follow Steps 2 and 3 for the raised buttonhole stitch (page 56), working the stitches around the outer edge of each chain stitch. To end the stitch, go down at **B**. Repeat for the stitches around the inner edge of each chain stitch.

3. Fill the center with French knot stitches (page 54).

Left-handed version: *Begin stitching on the chain stitch to the right of A.*

Barnacle Stitch

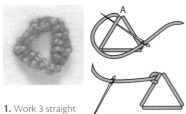

1. Work 3 straight stitches (page 43) as shown. Come up at **A**.

2. Follow Steps 2 and 3 of the raised buttonhole stitch (page 56), working the last stitch close to the first stitch.

Left-handed version: *Begin stitching on the straight stitch to the right of A.*

Knotted Seed Stitch

Stitch 3 French knot stitches (page 54) in a group. Repeat, filling in the section.

Variation: *Substitute a different knot stitch.*

Knotted Filler Shapes

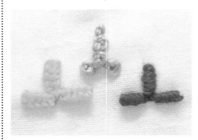

Bullion stitch

Raised buttonhole stitch

French knot stitch

Choose one of the templates and draw in the shape. Embroider with a stitch of your choice.

French Knot Stitch Flowers

1. Work a 3-wrap French Knot (page 54) for the center.

2. With the same thread or a different color, work 4–6 French knots, 2 wraps each, around the center in the order as shown, stitching close to the center or further away.

Variation: *Work with a different knot stitch.*

Spiderweb Rose Stitch

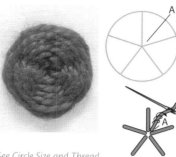

See Circle Size and Thread Choice (page 54).

1. Draw a circle and then draw 5 equally spaced spokes. Work straight stitches (page 43) from the outer edge of the circle to center as shown. Knot and cut the thread.

2. Thread a chenille needle with 30" (76.2cm) of your thread choice. Come up at **A**. *Note: If you are working with 2 or more threads, twirl the needle to the right to twist the threads.*

3. Weave the needle and thread over and under the spokes counterclockwise, pulling the thread through the spokes. To end the stitch, go down at **B**.

Left-handed version: *In Step 2, if using 2 or more threads, twirl the needle to the left to twist the threads. In Step 3, weave the stitches clockwise.*

Spiderweb Rose Stitch Variation

Follow the directions for the spiderweb rose (above), working with a color blend of threads for the petals.

Raised Spiderweb Stitch

1. Follow Step 1 of the spiderweb rose stitch (at left). Knot but do not cut the thread. Come up at **A**.

2. Work the outline stitch (page 47) over the spokes counterclockwise (but not through the fabric), pulling the thread around the spokes. To end the stitch, go down at **B**.

Note: *This stitch can be worked with 5 or more spokes.*

Left-handed version: *In Step 2, work the outline stitch clockwise.*

Jill's Flower Stitch

1. Follow the directions for the lazy daisy stitch flower (page 63) with 5 or 6 petals. Come up at **A**.

2. Follow the directions for the whip-stitch star (page 56) from Step 2, treating each lazy daisy stitch as a spoke. Work 3 rows around the center. To end the stitch, go down at **B**.

Chain-Stitch Rose

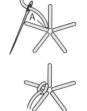

1. Follow Step 1 of the spiderweb rose stitch (at left). Knot but do not cut the thread. Come up at **A**.

2. Work the chain stitch (page 67) over the spokes counterclockwise (but not through the fabric), pulling the thread around the spokes. To end the stitch, go down at **B**.

Notes: *This stitch can be worked with 5 or more spokes.*

Left-handed version: *In Step 2, work the chain stitch clockwise.*

Tiny Dragonfly Stitch

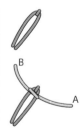

Body: Stitch 1 lazy daisy stitch (page 60).

Wings: Come up at **A**. Go under the lazy daisy stitch; then whip the thread over and then under again. Go down at **B**. Repeat for a total of 4 wings.

Eyes: Stitch 2 French knot stitches (page 54).

LAZY DAISY STITCHES

General Information

These individual stitches can be used as a single stitch, combined to create a border row, or added to another stitch to create a larger component.

The following stitches are formed by coming up at point **A** and then, in one motion, going down at point **B** and coming up at point **C**, which catches the loop formed by points **A** and **B**. The stitch would end with a point **D**. If the stitch has a detail, it would continue with point **E** and **F** stitches or more.

For a reference guide, use an erasable pen to draw a line or 2 points the length of the stitch.

Lazy Daisy Stitch

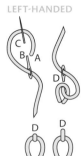

1. Come up at **A**. In one motion, go down at **B** and up at **C**. Wrap the working thread under the tip of the needle. Pull the needle through the fabric.

2. To end the stitch, go down at **D** or a short distance away for a long arm stitch.

Lazy Daisy Stitch Offset Base

Follow the directions for the lazy daisy stitch (at left), with point **B** higher and to the side of point **A**.

Double Lazy Daisy Stitch

1. Work 1 lazy daisy stitch with a long arm (at left).

2. Come up at **E**, thread the needle under the arm, and go down at **F**.

Left-handed version: *In Step 2, reverse* **E** *for* **F** *and vice versa.*

Berry Stitch

1. Work 1 lazy daisy stitch (above).

2. Come up directly below the first stitch and work a second longer stitch around the first stitch.

Lazy Daisy Stitch Twisted Base

1. Come up at **A**. In one motion, go down at **B** and up at **C**. Wrap the working thread over the needle and under the tip. Pull the needle through the fabric.

2. To end the stitch, go down at **D**.

Lazy Daisy Square Tip Stitch

LEFT-HANDED

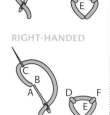

RIGHT-HANDED

1. Come up at **A**. In one motion, go down at **B** and up at **C**. Wrap the working thread under the tip of the needle. Gently pull the needle through the fabric, leaving a slight loop. Go down at **D** to catch one edge of the loop.

2. To end the stitch, come up at **E** and go down at **F** to catch the other edge of the loop.

Lazy Daisy with Bullion Tip Stitch

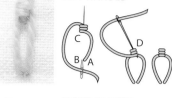

LEFT-HANDED

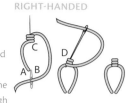

RIGHT-HANDED

1. Come up at **A**. In one motion, go down at **B** and up at **C**, but do not pull the thread through the fabric. Wrap the thread around the needle 2 or 3 times.

2. Pull the needle through the fabric. To end the stitch, go down at **D**, just beyond the wraps.

Lazy Daisy with Bullion Stitch

LEFT-HANDED

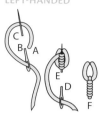

RIGHT-HANDED

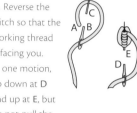

1. Follow Step 1 of the lazy daisy stitch (page 60).

2. Reverse the stitch so that the working thread is facing you. In one motion, go down at **D** and up at **E**, but do not pull the thread through the fabric.

3. Follow Step 2 of the bullion stitch (page 55), measuring the distance between **D** and **E**. Pull the wraps back toward you, keeping the wraps evenly spaced. To end the stitch, go down at **F**.

Note: *This stitch allows you to make a longer bullion stitch than in the lazy daisy with bullion tip stitch (above center).*

Lazy Daisy with French Knot Stitch

LEFT-HANDED   **RIGHT-HANDED**

1. Follow Step 1 of the lazy daisy stitch (page 60).

2. Holding the needle close to the fabric, wrap the thread 1–3 times around the needle. Go down at **D**. Pull the needle through the wrapped stitches and fabric.

Figure Eight Stitch

1. Come up at **A**. In one motion, go down at **B** and up at **C**; do not pull the needle through the fabric. Wrap the thread over the needle and under the tip; continue by wrapping the thread under the eye. Repeat 2 more times.

2. Place your thumb on the wraps, and pull the needle through the fabric. Go down at **D**.

3. To end the stitch, come up at **E** inside the bottom loop and down at **F**.

Optional: *Stitch a straight stitch (page 43) across the middle of the stitch.*

LEFT-HANDED

RIGHT-HANDED

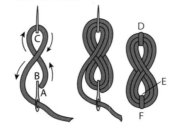
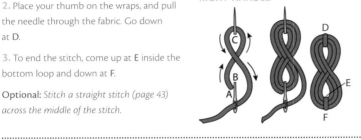

Lazy Daisy with Pistil Stitch

LEFT-HANDED

RIGHT-HANDED

1. Follow Step 1 of the lazy daisy stitch (page 60). Point **C** now becomes point **A**. Follow the directions for the pistil stitch (page 44), wrapping once.

2. Go down at **B**. Pull the needle and thread through the wrapped stitches and the fabric.

Lazy Daisy Plaited Stitch

LEFT-HANDED

1. Follow the directions for the lazy daisy stitch (page 60). *Come up at **A** and place the needle under the edge of the previous stitch.

2. Work a second lazy daisy stitch. Repeat from * to work a third stitch.

Optional: *More petals can be stitched to complete a flower.*

RIGHT-HANDED

Lazy Daisy Stitch Side-by-Side

1. Follow Step 1 of the lazy daisy stitch (page 60). *In one motion, go down at **B** (outside of, and longer than the previous stitch) and up at **C**.

2. Repeat from *, stitching a third loop the same size as the first stitch. To end the stitch, go down at **D**.

Left-handed version: *Work the stitches from right to left.*

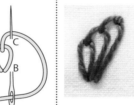

Looped Tendril Stitch

1. Follow Step 1 of the lazy daisy stitch (page 60). *In one motion, go down at **B** (outside of, and longer than the previous stitch) and up at **C**.

2. Repeat from *, stitching a third loop longer than the previous stitch. To end the stitch, go down at **D**.

Left-handed version: *Work the stitches from right to left.*

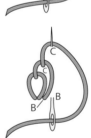

Lazy Daisy Stitch Crossed

1. Work 1 lazy daisy stitch (page 60) at an angle. Come up at **A**; *thread the needle under the first half of the stitch and over the second half of the stitch.

2. Repeat from *. In one motion, go down at **B** and up at **C** with the loop under the tip of the needle. Pull the thread through the fabric. To end the stitch, go down at **D**.

Pin Rose Stitch

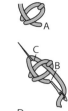

1. Follow Step 1 of the lazy daisy stitch (page 60), wrapping the working thread under needle. Wrap the thread a second and third time.

2. Place your thumb on the wraps; pull the needle through the fabric. Go down at **D**.

2. To end the stitch, come up at **E** inside the loop and down at **F**.

Lazy Daisy Piggyback Stitch

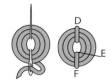

Follow Step 1 of the lazy daisy stitch (page 60). Work a smaller stitch on the tip of and inside the first stitch. To end the stitch, go down at **D**.

Russian Chain Stitch

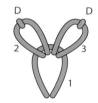

Follow Step 1 of the lazy daisy stitch (page 60). Work a smaller lazy daisy stitch inside the first stitch to one side. Work another stitch on the other side.

Lazy Daisy Stitch Flowers

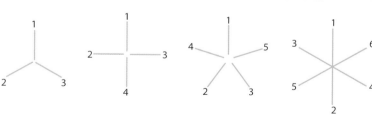

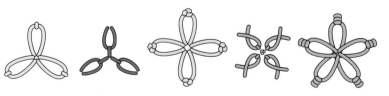

1. Choose a template and draw in the lines.

2. Work the petals in the order they are shown.

- Petal suggestions: Lazy daisy stitch (page 60), lazy daisy stitch with long arm (page 60), lazy daisy with French knot stitch (page 61), lazy daisy stitch twisted base (page 60), lazy daisy with bullion tip stitch (page 61), berry stitch (page 60), lazy daisy stitch with long arm (page 60), or lazy daisy square tip (page 61)

Optional: *Work a French knot stitch (page 54) or other knotted stitch in the center of the flower.*

Lazy Daisy Stitch with Center Stitches

Center stitch: Work one of the following stitches: straight stitch (page 43), 3 French knot stitches (page 54), or 1 bullion stitch (page 55).

Petal: Work 1 lazy daisy stitch (page 60) over the center stitch.

Sunflower Stitch

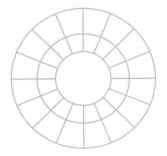

1. Draw 3 graduated circles. Draw in equally spaced marks for the petals.

• **Petals:** Work 1 lazy daisy stitch with bullion stitch (page 61) for each petal.

  Note: *Begin the lazy daisy stitch at the inner circle, stopping at the middle circle. Work the bullion portion of the stitch using the outer circle.*

• **Center:** Work 3-wrap French knot stitches (page 54) in the center.

Iris Stitch

Work 1 lazy daisy stitch (page 60). Come up at **A**, pass the needle under the bottom of the stitch, and go down at **B**.

Left-handed version: *Reverse **A** for **B** and vice versa.*

Lazy Daisy Tulip Stitch

Center: Work 1 lazy daisy stitch (page 60).

Sides: Come up at **A**. In one motion, go down at **B** and up at **C**; pull the needle through the fabric. To end the stitch, go down at **D**. Repeat for the other side.

Lazy Daisy Heart Stitch

Center: Work 1 lazy daisy stitch (page 60).

Sides: Come up at **A**. In one motion, go down at **B** and up at **C**; pull the needle through the fabric. To end the stitch, go down at **D**. Repeat for the other side.

Lazy Daisy Triangle Stitch

Center: Work 1 lazy daisy stitch (page 60).

Sides: Come up at **A**. In one motion, go down at **B** and up at **C**; pull the needle through the fabric. To end the stitch, go down at **D**. Repeat for the other side.

Butterfly Stitch

Body: Stitch 1 lazy daisy with bullion tip stitch (page 61).

Wings: Stitch 2 looped tendril stitches (page 62).

Antennae and legs: Stitch 2 straight stitches (page 43) for each.

Dragonfly Stitch

Draw the lines for the body and the wings.

Body: Stitch 1 lazy daisy stitch (page 60). Stitch 3 straight stitches (page 43) across the body as shown.

Wings: Stitch 4 lazy daisy stitches.

Eyes: Stitch 2 French knot stitches (page 54).

Bumblebee Stitch

Draw the lines for the body and the wings.

Body: Stitch 1 berry stitch (page 60).

Wings: Stitch 4 berry stitches.

Antennae and legs: Stitch 2 straight stitches (page 43) for each.

Bud with Calyx Stitch

Bud: Stitch 1 lazy daisy stitch (page 60).

Calyx: Stitch 1 fly stitch (page 92) over the bud.

Bud with Knotted Calyx Stitch

Bud: Work 1 lazy daisy stitch (page 60).

Calyx: Come up at **A**. Thread the needle under the bottom of the bud, and wrap the working thread under the tip of the needle. Pull the needle through the stitch. To end the stitch, go down at **B**.

Left-handed version: *Begin point **A** and end point **B** on the right side of the stitch.*

Bud Vine

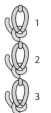

1

2

3

Bud with knotted calyx stitch (page 65)

1

2

3

Bud with calyx stitch (page 65)

Work the stitches starting at the top of the row.

Palm Leaf Stitch

1. Work 1 lazy daisy stitch (page 60).

2. **Sides:** Beginning at the top of the first stitch, come up at **A**. In one motion, go down at **B** and up at **C**; pull the needle through the fabric. Work a second and third stitch. To end the stitch, go down at **D**.

3. Repeat Step 2 for the other side of the lazy daisy stitch.

4. Work a row of stem stitches (page 47) for the stem.

Lazy Daisy Stitch Stalks

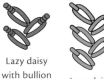

Lazy daisy stitch

Lazy daisy with bullion tip stitch

Lazy daisy long arm and lazy daisy with French knot stitch

1. Draw in the stalk template A (page 46).

2. Work the stitches in the order that they are listed.

Variations: *Change the stalk or the length of the stitches, substitute a different stitch, or use a different thread every other stitch.*

Lazy Daisy Stitch Rows

Double row

Single row   **Plaited row**

Single row: Work the stitches in a straight row, beginning the next stitch at the tip of the previous stitch.

Double row: Work the stitches in different directions, grouping 2 together.

Plaited row: Work the first stitch; work the consecutive stitches beginning in the previous stitch.

Stitch suggestions: Lazy daisy with French knot stitch, lazy daisy stitch, lazy daisy stitch twisted base.

Variations: *Change the length of the stitches or substitute a different stitch.*

CHAIN STITCHES

General Information

These continuous stitches can be used for a border row or to create a shape. After the stitch is formed, individual stitches can be added to the tips or around the base to create a larger design.

The following stitches are formed by coming up at point **A** and then, in one motion, going down at point **B** and coming up at point **C**, which catches the loop formed by points **A** and **B**. Point **C** becomes point **A** for the following stitch. The stitch is work continuously and would end at point **D**. If the stitch has a detail it would continue with point **E** and **F** stitches or more.

For a reference guide and even spacing, you could draw a line with an erasable pen and then mark the line at even intervals.

Chain Stitch

LEFT-HANDED

RIGHT-HANDED

1. Come up at **A**. *In one motion, go down at **B** and up at **C**. Wrap the working thread under the tip of the needle. Pull the needle through the fabric.

2. Repeat from * to finish the row, starting inside the previous loop. To finish the stitch, go down at **D**.

Chain Stitch Cable

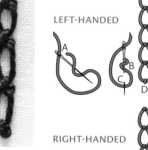

LEFT-HANDED

RIGHT-HANDED

1. Come up at **A**. *Wrap the thread over the needle once.

2. In one motion, go down at **B** and up at **C**. Wrap the working thread under the tip of the needle, and pull the knot close to the fabric. Pull the thread through the fabric.

3. Repeat from * to finish the row. To end the stitch, go down at **D**.

Chain Stitch Laced or Whipped

Chain stitch laced   Chain stitch whipped

1. Stitch a row of chain stitches (at left).

2. With a different color or type of thread, come up next to the first stitch in the row. Follow the directions for the laced or whipped version of the stitch below.

• **Laced:** Slide the needle under each stitch, working above or below them, creating a short loop between stitches.

• **Whipped:** Slide the needle under the stitch and then over the stitch. Repeat for each stitch.

3. To end the stitch, go down next to the last stitch in the row.

Chain Stitch Zigzag

Follow the directions for the chain stitch (page 67), angling the first stitch away from the seam and the next stitch toward the seam. Repeat the pattern across the row.

Note: *You can use vine template B (page 51) for accurate spacing.*

Chain Stitch Netted

1. Stitch 1 row of chain stitch zigzag stitches (at left). Turn the fabric.

2. Stitch a second row, with the spokes mirroring the first.

Variations: *Change the length, the type of the stitch, or the color of thread in the second row.*

Chain Stitch Feathered

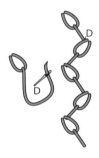

1. Follow Step 1 of the chain stitch (page 67), angling the stitch away from the seam. Go down at D, a short distance away.

2. Stitch the next stitch beginning at D of the previous stitch. Repeat Steps 1 and 2, angling the stitches from side to side.

Chain Stitch Feathered Netted

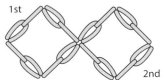

1. Stitch 1 row of chain stitch feathered stitches (above right).

2. Stitch a second row, with the spokes mirroring the first.

Variations: *Change the length of the stitch or color of the thread in the second row.*

Chain Stitch with Raised Buttonhole Stitch

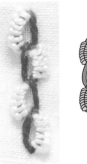

1. Stitch 1 row of chain stitches (page 67).

2. With a different color of thread, come up next to the first stitch in the row. Follow Steps 2 and 3 of the raised buttonhole stitch (page 56), working over one side of the first stitch.

3. Repeat Step 2 to finish the row, alternating sides on the chain stitch row.

Chain Stitch Open Tip

LEFT-HANDED

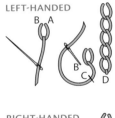

RIGHT-HANDED

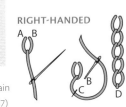

1. Work a chain stitch (page 67) with points **A** and **B** slightly apart. *In one motion, go down at **B** (outside the previous loop) and up at **C**.

2. Repeat from * to finish the row. To end the stitch, go down at **D**.

Chain Stitch Open with Knot Tip

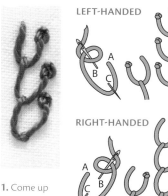

LEFT-HANDED

RIGHT-HANDED

1. Come up at **A**. *Loop the thread over your finger and place the loop next to the fabric. Backstitch the needle in one motion down at an angle at **B** through the loop and up at **C**. Pull the thread tightly; then pull the needle through the fabric.

2. Repeat from * to finish the row. To finish the stitch, go down at **D**.

Chain Stitch Spiny

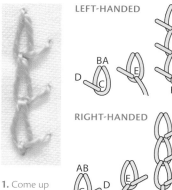

LEFT-HANDED

RIGHT-HANDED

1. Come up at **A**. Follow Step 1 of the chain stitch (page 67) from *. Go down at **D**, angling up. Come up at **E**, which now becomes **A** of the chain stitch.

2. Repeat from * to finish the row, working a spine outside each chain. To end the stitch, do down at **F**.

Variation: *Alternate the spine every other stitch.*

Chain Stitch with Picot

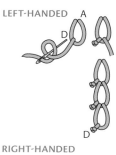

LEFT-HANDED

RIGHT-HANDED

1. Come up at **A**. Follow Step 1 of the chain stitch (page 67) from *. Follow the directions for Chinese knot stitch (page 55) from Step 2, going down at **D**, to the side of the chain stitch.

2. Repeat Step 1 above from * to finish the row, starting inside the previous loop.

Chain Stitch with Loop Stitch

LEFT-HANDED

RIGHT-HANDED

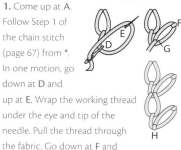

1. Come up at **A**. Follow Step 1 of the chain stitch (page 67) from *. In one motion, go down at **D** and up at **E**. Wrap the working thread under the eye and tip of the needle. Pull the thread through the fabric. Go down at **F** and come up at **G**.

2. Repeat from * to finish the row. To end the stitch, go down at **H**.

Rope Stitch

LEFT-HANDED

RIGHT-HANDED

1. Come up at **A**. *In one motion, and directly below **A**, go down at **B** and up at **C**. Wrap the working thread under the tip of the needle. Pull the needle through the fabric.

2. Repeat from * to finish the row, with **B** outside and close to the edge of the previous stitch. To end the stitch, go down at **D**.

Chain Stitch Twisted

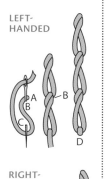

LEFT-HANDED

RIGHT-HANDED

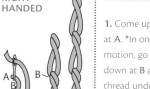

1. Come up at **A**. *In one motion, go down at **B** and up at **C**. Wrap the working thread under the tip of the needle. Pull the needle through the fabric.

2. Repeat from * to finish the row. To end the stitch, go down at **D**.

Chain Stitch Twisted and Feather Stitch

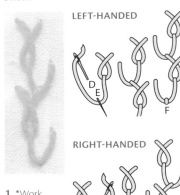

LEFT-HANDED

RIGHT-HANDED

1. *Work a twisted chain stitch (page 69). In one motion, go down at **D** and up at **E**. Wrap the working thread under the tip of the needle. Pull the needle through the fabric.

2. Repeat from * to finish the row. To end the stitch, go down at **F** after either stitch in Step 1.

Open Chain Stitch

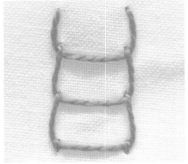

LEFT-HANDED

RIGHT-HANDED

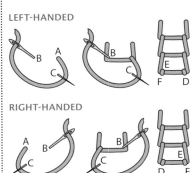

Work this stitch between 2 parallel lines.

1. Come up at **A**. *In one motion, go down at **B** and up at **C**. Pull the needle through the fabric, leaving a slight loop.

2. Repeat from * to finish the row, working **B** into the previous stitch. To end the stitch, go down at **D**. Come up at **E** and down at **F**.

Open Chain Stitch Double Row

LEFT-HANDED

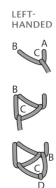

RIGHT-HANDED

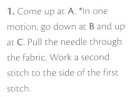

Work this stitch between 2 parallel lines.

1. Come up at **A**. *In one motion, go down at **B** and up at **C**. Pull the needle through the fabric. Work a second stitch to the side of the first stitch.

2. Repeat from * to finish the row, beginning inside the previous loop and working the stitches from side to side. To end the stitch, go down at **D**.

Chain Stitch Double

LEFT-HANDED

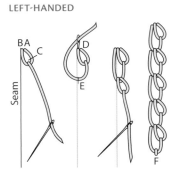

RIGHT-HANDED

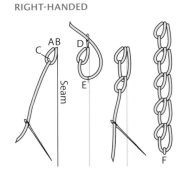

1. *Follow the directions for the chain stitch (page 67), working the stitch slightly angled from the seam.

2. In one motion, go down at **D** next to **B** and up at **E** on the seam.

3. To finish the row, repeat from *, beginning in the loop of the previous stitch. To end the stitch, go down at **F**.

Chain Stitch with Up-and-Down Stitch

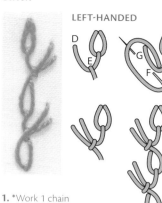

LEFT-HANDED

1. *Work 1 chain stitch (page 67). In one motion, go down at **D** and up at **E**. Pull the thread through the fabric.

2. In one motion, go down at **F** and up at **G**. Loop the working thread over the tip of the needle. Pull the needle through the fabric. Thread the needle under the loop and gently pull the thread to tighten.

3. To finish the row, repeat from *. To end the stitch, go down at **H**.

RIGHT-HANDED

Chain Shell Stitch

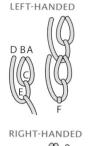

LEFT-HANDED

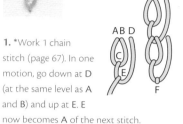

RIGHT-HANDED

1. *Work 1 chain stitch (page 67). In one motion, go down at **D** (at the same level as **A** and **B**) and up at **E**. **E** now becomes **A** of the next stitch.

2. To finish the row, repeat from *. To end the stitch, go down at **F**.

Chain Shell Stitch Variation

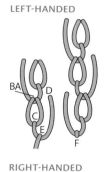

LEFT-HANDED

RIGHT-HANDED

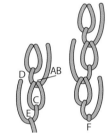

Follow the directions for the chain shell stitch (at left), working the stitches from side to side.

Chain Stitch with Open Chain-Stitch Edge

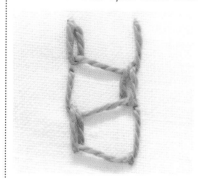

LEFT-HANDED   **RIGHT-HANDED**

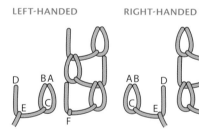

1. *Work 1 chain stitch (page 67). In one motion, go down at **D** and up at **E**. Point **E** now becomes point **A** of the chain stitch.

2. To finish the row, repeat from *, working the stitches from side to side. To end the stitch, go down at **F**.

Waved Chain Stitch

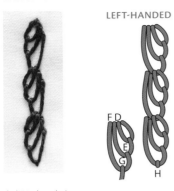

LEFT-HANDED

RIGHT-HANDED

1. *Work 1 chain stitch (page 67) slightly angled. Work a second stitch from **D** to **E**, slightly below and longer than the first stitch. Work a third stitch from **F** to **G**, slightly below and longer than the second stitch.

2. Repeat from *
to finish the row, beginning in the last loop of the previous stitch. To end the stitch, go down at **H**.

Chain Stitch Short-Long

Follow the directions for the chain stitch (page 67), working a pattern of 1 short stitch and then 1 long stitch.

Variations: *Change the pattern to 2 short stitches and 1 long stitch; or change the size to small, medium, and large or some other combination.*

Open Chain Stitch with Details

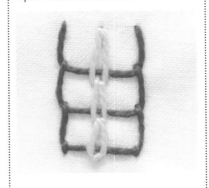

Stitch 1 row of open chain stitches (page 70). With a different color of thread, work a row of chain stitches (page 67) down the center of the first row.

Variations: *Work a different detail stitch.*

Chain Stitch Double Zigzag

1. Follow Steps 1 and 2 of the chain stitch double (page 70), with both stitches angled.

2. Repeat, with the next set of stitches angled in the opposite direction.

3. Repeat Steps 1 and 2 above to finish the row.

F

Chain Stitch with Open Chain-Stitch Edge Variation

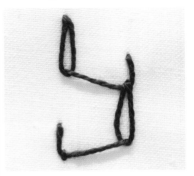

Follow the directions for the chain stitch with open chain-stitch edge (page 71), changing the length of the stitches.

Magic Chain Stitch

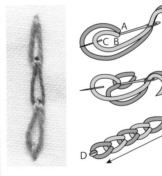

1. Thread the needle with 2 colors of the same thread. Knot the tails together.

2. Come up at **A**. Follow Step 1 of the chain stitch (page 67) from *, wrapping one color of thread under the needle. As you pull the needle through the fabric, the second color will disappear to the back.

3. Repeat from * to finish the row, alternating the thread color. To end the stitch, go down at **D**. Both threads will catch the end of the stitch.

Chain and Cross Stitches

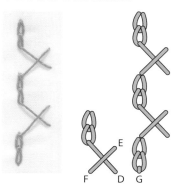

1. *Work 2 chain stitches (page 67). Go down at **D**. Come up at **E** and go down at **F**.

2. Repeat from * to finish the row. To finish the stitch, go down at **F** or **G**.

Chain Stitch Vines

Chain stitch (page 67)

Chain and stem stitches (below)

Draw in the vine. Embroider with the stitch of your choice.

Chain Stitch with Variations

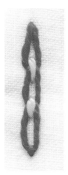

Chain and straight stitches

Stitch 1 row of chain stitches (page 67). Stitch a row of straight stitches (page 43) inside the chain stitches.

Chain and stem stitches

Work 1 chain stitch (page 67); work 3 stem stitches (page 47). Repeat the pattern to finish the row.

BARB STITCHES

General Information

These individual stitches can be used as a single stitch, combined to create a border row, or added to another stitch to create a larger component.

The following stitches are formed by coming up at point **A** and then, in one motion, going down at point **B** and coming up at point **C**, which catches the loop formed by points **A** and **B**. The stitch would end with a point **D**. If the stitch has a detail, it would continue with point **E** and **F** stitches or more.

For a reference guide, use an erasable pen to draw 2 parallel lines the length and width of the stitch.

Barb Stitch

LEFT-HANDED

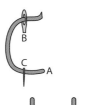

1. Come up at **A**. In one motion, go down at **B** and up at **C**. Wrap the working thread under the tip of the needle. Pull the needle through the fabric.

2. To end the stitch, go down at **D** or a short distance away.

RIGHT-HANDED

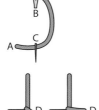

Barb Stitch Angled

LEFT-HANDED

Follow the directions for the barb stitch (at left), with **B** and **C** angled back toward **A**.

Variations: *Alter the height or the length of the stitch.*

RIGHT-HANDED

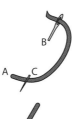

Barb Stitch with Knot Tip

LEFT-HANDED

1. Come up at **A**. *Loop the thread over your finger and place the loop next to the fabric. Backstitch the needle in one motion down at an angle at **B** through the loop and up at **C**. Pull the thread tightly; then pull the needle through the fabric.

RIGHT-HANDED

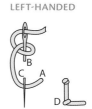

2. To end the stitch, go down at **D**.

Barb Stitch with Picot Stitch

LEFT-HANDED

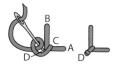

RIGHT-HANDED

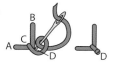

1. Follow Step 1 of the barb stitch (previous page).

2. Follow the directions for the Chinese knot stitch (page 55) from Step 2, going down at **D**, to the side of the stitch.

Barb Stitch Looped

LEFT-HANDED

RIGHT-HANDED

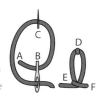

1. Come up at **A**. In one motion, go down at **B** and up at **C**. Wrap the working thread under the eye and the tip of the needle and back to the base of the stitch. Pull the needle through the fabric. Go down at **D**.

2. To end the stitch, come up at **E** and go down at **F**.

Barb Stitch with Twisted Loop

LEFT-HANDED

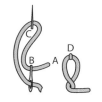

RIGHT-HANDED

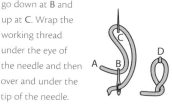

1. Come up at **A**. In one motion, go down at **B** and up at **C**. Wrap the working thread under the eye of the needle and then over and under the tip of the needle. Pull the needle through the fabric. Go down at **D**.

2. Or follow Step 2 for the barb stitch looped (at left).

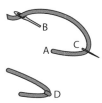

Barb Stitch Capped

1. Follow the directions for the barb stitch (previous page).

2. Come up at **E** and down at **F**.

Barb Stitch with Arrow Tip Detail

1. Follow the directions for the barb stitch (previous page).

2. Work a straight stitch (page 43) from **E** to **F** on either side of the tip.

Boomerang Stitch

LEFT-HANDED

RIGHT-HANDED

1. Come up at **A**. In one motion, go down at **B** (above and to the side of **A**) and up at **C**. Wrap the working thread under the tip of the needle. Pull the needle through the fabric.

2. To end the stitch, go down at **D**.

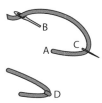

Barb Stitch Up and Down

LEFT-HANDED

RIGHT-HANDED

1. Follow Step 1 of the barb stitch (page 74). In one motion, go down at **D** and up at **E**. Loop the working thread over the tip of the needle.

2. Pull the needle through the fabric. Thread the needle under the loop and gently pull the thread to tighten.

3. To end the stitch, go down at **F**.

Barbed Wire Stitch

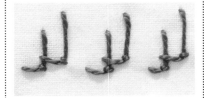

LEFT-HANDED

RIGHT-HANDED

1. Follow the directions for the barb stitch (page 74).

2. Work a second stitch above it, crossing over the straight potion of the previous stitch.

3. Repeat Steps 1 and 2 to finish the row.

Barbed Wire Stitch Variation

LEFT-HANDED

RIGHT-HANDED

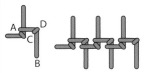

1. Follow the directions for the barb stitch (page 74).

2. Work a second stitch upside down, crossing over the straight potion of the previous stitch.

3. Repeat Step 1, crossing over the straight portion of the previous stitch, and Step 2, to finish the row.

Crossed Wire Stitch

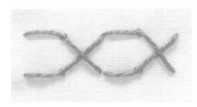

LEFT-HANDED

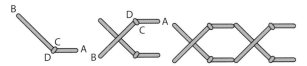

RIGHT-HANDED

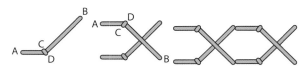

1. Follow the directions for the barb stitch angled (page 74).

2. Work a second stitch above it, crossing over the angled portion of the stitch.

3. Repeat Steps 1 and 2 to finish the row.

Barb Stitches Crossed

Barb stitch angled (page 74)

Barb stitch angled, different lengths

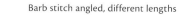
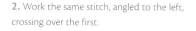

1. Work a barb stitch, listed above, angled to the right.

2. Work the same stitch, angled to the left, crossing over the first.

Variations: *Change the stitch length, or work the second stitch in a different color.*

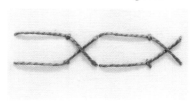

Barb stitch with knot tip (page 74)

Barb stitch capped (page 75)

Crossed Wire Stitch Elongated

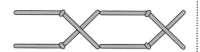

Follow the directions for the crossed wire stitch (page 76), elongating the first part of the stitch.

Crossed Wire Stitch Variation

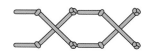

Follow the directions for the crossed wire stitch (page 76), substituting the barb stitch with knot tip (page 74).

Barb Stitch Looped Crossed

Work a right-handed version of the barb stitch looped (page 75) and angled. Work a left-handed version of the barb stitch angled (page 74), crossing over the first.

Optional: *Work a straight stitch (page 43) across the middle of the 2 stitches.*

Santa Fe Star Stitch

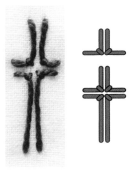

1. Work 2 barb stitches (page 74) close together: 1 right-handed and 1 left-handed.

2. Repeat Step 1, but working the stitches upside down and longer.

Fireworks Stitch

1. Draw a half-circle and mark off in sections.

2. Work the barb stitch (page 74), right-handed or left-handed, with the tip (point **B**) in the center of the bottom edge.

Dandelion Stitch

1. Draw a circle with a smaller circle in the center.

2. Work the barb stitch (page 74), right-handed or left-handed, with the tip ending at the smaller circle in the center.

3. Work the pistil stitch (page 44) between each barb stitch, starting at the inner circle with the tip worked in random lengths beyond the outer circle.

Optional: Work seed stitches (page 46) in the center of the flower.

Wind Stitch

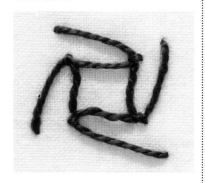

Work 4 boomerang stitches (page 75), right-handed or left-handed, in the order shown.

Tiny Butterfly Stitch

Work 1 right-handed version of the barb stitch looped (page 75) and angled. Work 1 left-handed version, crossing over the first.

Little Fly Stitch

Body: Stitch 1 straight stitch (page 43).

Wings: Stitch 1 right-handed and left-handed boomerang stitch (page 75).

Barb Stitch Flowers

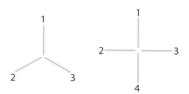

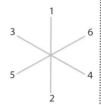

1. Choose a template and draw in the lines.

2. Work the petals in the order they are shown.

• **Petal suggestions:** Barb stitch (page 74), barb stitch looped (page 75), barb stitch with knot tip (page 74), or barb stitch with picot stitch (page 75)

Optional: *Work a French knot stitch (page 54) or other knotted stitch in the center of the flower.*

Barb Stitch Stalks

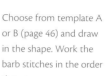

Choose from template A or B (page 46) and draw in the shape. Work the barb stitches in the order shown.

Variations: *Change the length of the stitches or substitute a different stitch.*

Barb Stitch Grouped Row

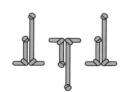

Barb stitch with knot tip (page 74)

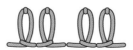

Barb stitch looped (page 75)

Following the directions for the barb stitch listed above, work a right-handed version and then a left-handed version.

Variations: *Change the length of the stitches or substitute a different stitch.*

Barb Stitch Random Netting

Follow the directions for the barb stitch (page 74). Randomly work the stitches upside down to fill in a section.

Variations: *Change the length or type of the stitch.*

BLANKET AND BUTTONHOLE STITCHES

General Information

These continuous stitches can be used for a border row or to create a shape. After the stitch is formed, individual stitches can be added to the tips or around the base to create a larger design.

The following stitches are formed by coming up at point **A** and then, in one motion, going down at point **B** and coming up at point **C**, which catches the loop formed by points **A** and **B**. Point **C** becomes point **A** for the following stitch. The stitch is work continuously and would end at point **D**. If the stitch has a detail, it would continue with point **E** and **F** stitches or more.

For a reference guide and even spacing, use an erasable pen to draw 2 parallel lines the length and width of the row; then mark off the lines at even intervals.

Blanket Stitch

1. Come up at **A**. *In one motion, go down at **B** and up at **C**. Wrap the working thread under the tip of the needle. Pull the needle through the fabric.

2. Repeat from * to finish the row. To end the stitch, go down at **D** or a short distance away.

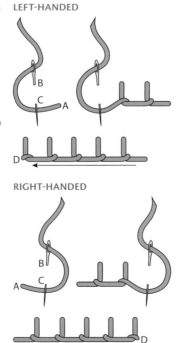

LEFT-HANDED

RIGHT-HANDED

Blanket Stitch Height and Spacing Variations

Follow the steps of the blanket stitch (at left), varying the height and space between the spokes.

Short-medium-long-medium-short

Tiny-short-medium-long-longer

Short-long

Short-long-short

Even

Short-long, short-short-long

Spaced

Short-medium-long

Even grouped

Blanket Stitch Zipper

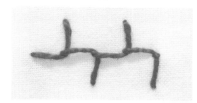

LEFT-HANDED

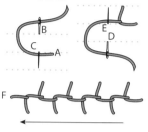

RIGHT-HANDED

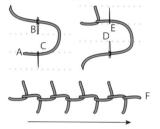

Work the tips of the stitch on the 2 outer lines and the base of the stitch along the middle line.

1. *Work 1 blanket stitch (previous page).

2. Go down at **D** and up at **E**, wrapping the working thread under the tip of the needle. Pull the needle through the fabric.

3. Repeat Steps 1 and 2 to finish the row, alternating the direction of the stitches. To end the stitch, go down at **F**.

Variations: *Change the length or spacing of the stitches.*

Even

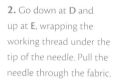

Short-long

Grouped

Blanket Stitch Up and Down

LEFT-HANDED

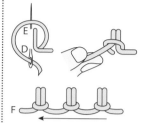

RIGHT-HANDED

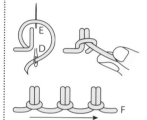

1. *Work 1 blanket stitch (previous page). In one motion, go down at **D** and up at **E**. Loop the working thread over the tip of the needle.

2. Pull the needle through the fabric. Thread the needle under the loop and gently pull the thread to tighten.

3. Repeat from * to finish the row. To end the stitch, go down at **F**.

Variations: *Change the length of the stitches or the angle of the stitches.*

Even

Short-long

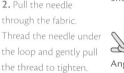

Angle-straight

Blanket Stitch Locked Zipper

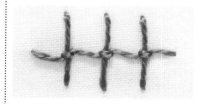

LEFT-HANDED

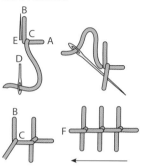

RIGHT-HANDED

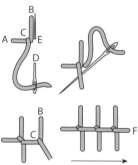

1. *Work 1 blanket stitch (previous page). In one motion, go down at **D** and up at **E**. Gently pull the thread through the fabric. Pass the needle under the stitch and tighten the thread.

2. Repeat from * to finish the row. To end the stitch, go down at **F**.

Blanket Stitch with Loose Knot Stitch

LEFT-HANDED

RIGHT-HANDED

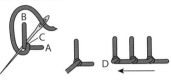

Short-long-short

Blanked stitch looped

Blanket stitch closed

1. *Work 1 blanket stitch (page 80). Go under the base stitch only; wrap the working thread under the tip of the needle. Pull the thread firmly around the base stitch.

2. Repeat from * to finish the row. To end the stitch, go down at **D**.

Variations: *Add this knot to any of the blanket stitch directions.*

Blanket Stitch Looped

LEFT-HANDED

RIGHT-HANDED

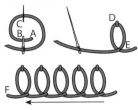

1. Come up at **A**. *In one motion, go down at **B** and up at **C**. Wrap the working thread under the eye and the tip of the needle and back to the base of the stitch. Pull the needle through the fabric.

2. Go down at **D** to catch the loop. Come up at **E**.

3. Repeat from * to finish the stitch. To end the stitch, go down at **F**.

Variations: *Change the length, spacing, or number of stitches in a pattern.*

Blanket Stitch Angled

LEFT-HANDED

RIGHT-HANDED

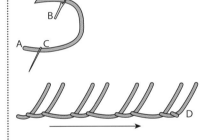

1. Come up at **A**. Follow Step 1 of the blanket stitch (page 80) from *, with the stitch angled.

2. Repeat from * to finish the row. To end the stitch, go down at **D**.

Variations: *Change the spacing or pattern of the stitches.*

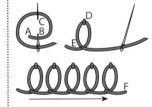

Even

Grouped

Right-left

Blanket Stitch with Twisted Loop

LEFT-HANDED

RIGHT-HANDED

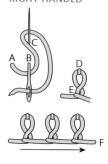

1. Come up at **A**. *In one motion, go down at **B** and up at **C**. Wrap the working thread under the eye of the needle and then over and under the tip of the needle and back to the base. Pull the needle through the fabric.

2. Go down at **D** to catch the loop. Come up at **E**.

3. Repeat from * to finish the stitch. To end the stitch, go down at **F**.

Blanket Stitch Looped Zipper

LEFT-HANDED

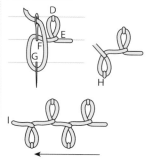

RIGHT-HANDED

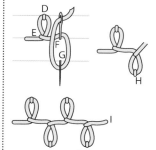

Work the looped portion of the stitch on the 2 outer lines and the base of the stitch along the middle line.

1. Follow Step 1 of the blanket stitch looped (previous page).

2. Go down at **F** and up at **G**. Wrap the working thread under the eye and then the tip of the needle to the base of the stitch. Pull the needle through the fabric. Go down at **H** to catch the loop.

3. Repeat Steps 1 and 2 to finish the row, alternating the direction of the stitches. To end the stitch, go down at **I**.

Blanket Stitch Whipped or with Buttonhole Stitch

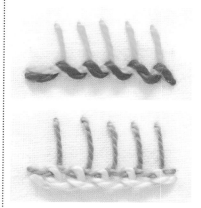

Whipped

Buttonhole stitch

1. Stitch a row of blanket stitches (page 80).

2. With a different color or type of thread, come up next to the first stitch in the row. Follow the directions below for each stitch. To end the stitch, go down next to the last stitch in the row.

- **Whipped:** Slide the needle under the stitch and then over the stitch. Repeat for each stitch.

- **Buttonhole stitch:** Follow Steps 2 and 3 for the raised buttonhole stitch (page 56), working 1 stitch into each blanket stitch.

Blanket Stitch Angled Variations

Follow the directions for the blanket stitch angled (page 82), working the stitches within 3 more lines.

Short-long

Short-long-short

Angle-straight-angle

Variations:
Change the length, spacing, or number of stitches in a pattern.

Blanket Stitch Mirrored

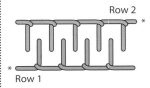

A. Tips mirrored

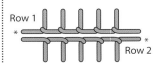

B. Bottom edge mirrored

1. Stitch 1 row of blanket stitches (page 80), beginning the row at *. Turn the fabric.

A. Stitch a row with the spokes worked into the first row, beginning at *.

B. Stitch a row with the base close to the first row, beginning at *.

Blanket Stitch Closed

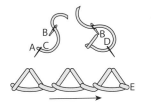

Even

Closed-straight

Follow the directions for the blanket stitch angled (page 82).

1. Work 1 stitch angled to the right.

2. Work a second stitch angled to the left, going down at **B** and up at **D**.

3. Repeat Steps 1 and 2 to finish the row. To end the stitch, go down at **E**.

Variations: *Change the spacing or add in additional stitches.*

Blanket Stitch Crossed

Even

Long arm-short arm

1. *Work 1 blanket stitch angled (page 82). Work 1 blanket stitch angled to the left, going down at **D** and up at **E**, crossing over the previous stitch.

2. Repeat Step 1 to finish the row. To end the stitch, go down at **F**.

Variation: *Change the length of the stitches.*

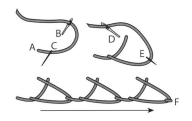

Blanket Stitch Closed with Details

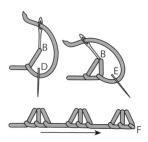

Follow the directions for the blanket stitch angled (page 82) and the blanket stitch (page 80).

1. Come up at **A**. Work 1 blanket stitch angled to the right. Work 1 straight blanket stitch, going down at **B** and up at **D**. Work 1 blanket stitch angled to the left, going down at **B** and up at **E**.

2. Repeat Step 1 finish the row. To end the stitch, go down at **F**.

Blanket Stitch Closed or Crossed Variations

Closed

Crossed

Straight-angle

Crossed, straight, straight, crossed

Angle-straight-straight-angle

Angle-long-angle

Crossed small, crossed big

Angle-straight

Follow the directions for the stitches using 1 or more of the following directions: Blanket stitch (page 80), blanket stitch closed (previous page), blanket stitch closed with details (at left), blanket stitch crossed (previous page), or blanket stitch angled (page 82).

Blanket Stitch with Knot Tip

1. Come up at **A**. *Loop the thread over your finger and place the loop next to the fabric. Backstitch the needle in one motion down at an angle at **B** through the loop and up at **C**. Pull the thread tightly; then pull the needle through the fabric.

2. Repeat from * to finish the row. To finish the stitch, go down at **D**.

Variation: *Change the length of the stitches.*

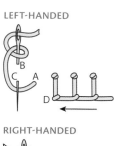

LEFT-HANDED

RIGHT-HANDED

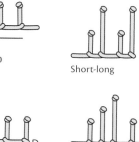

Even

Short-long

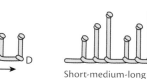

Short-medium-long

Blanket Stitch with Knot Tip Angled

LEFT-HANDED

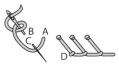

RIGHT-HANDED

Follow the steps for the blanket stitch with knot tip (page 85), angling the stitch as shown.

Variations: *Change the length of the stitches or the combination of the stitches.*

Short-long

Right-left pattern

Closed-crossed

Shell Stitch

LEFT-HANDED

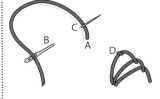

RIGHT-HANDED

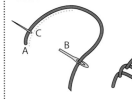

1. Draw or follow a quarter-circle. Follow Step 1 of the blanket stitch (page 80), with **A** and **C** on the curved line.

2. Work a second stitch and a third stitch along the curved line. To end the stitch, go down at **D**.

Blanket Mock Sheaf Stitch

1. Work 1 blanket stitch angled (page 82) to the right: **A**, **B**, and **C**. Work a straight blanket stitch (page 80), straight crossing over the first stitch: **C**, **D**, and **E**. Work a blanket stitch angled to the left, crossing over the previous stitches: **E**, **F**, and **G**.

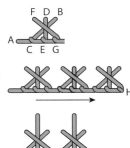

2. Repeat Step 1 to finish the row. To end the stitch, go down at **H**.

Optional: *Work a straight stitch (page 43) over each crossed section with the same or a different color of thread.*

Variation: *Change the length of the stitches.*

Shell Stitch Row

1. Work 1 shell stitch (above center).

2. Work a second stitch upside down and to the right with **A** of the new stitch close to **B** of the previous stitch.

3. Repeat Steps 1 and 2 to finish the row.

Blanket Stitch with Picot Stitch

1. *Work 1 blanket stitch (page 80). Follow the directions for the Chinese knot stitch (page 55) from Step 2, going down at **D**, to the side of the stitch. Come up at **E**.

2. Repeat from * above to finish the row. To end the stitch, go down at **F**.

LEFT-HANDED

RIGHT-HANDED

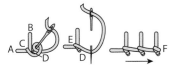

Magic Blanket Stitch

LEFT-HANDED

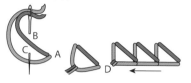

RIGHT-HANDED

1. Thread the needle with 2 colors of the same thread. Knot the tails together.

2. Come up at **A**. Follow Step 1 of the blanket stitch (page 80) from *, and wrap one color of thread under the needle. As you pull the needle through the fabric, the second color will create an angled stitch.

3. Repeat from * to finish the row. To end the stitch, go down at **D**. Both threads will catch the end of the stitch.

Blanket and Lazy Daisy Stitches

LEFT-HANDED

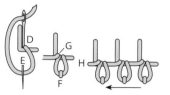

RIGHT-HANDED

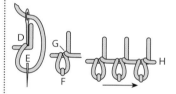

1. Work 1 blanket stitch (page 80). Work 1 lazy daisy stitch (page 60), going down at **D** and up at **E**; then go down at **F**. Come up at **G**.

2. Repeat Step 1 to finish the row. To end the stitch, go down at **H**.

Variations: *Change the number of blanket stitches or the type of blanket stitch.*

Blanket and Pistil Stitches

LEFT-HANDED   **RIGHT-HANDED**

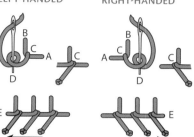

1. Work 1 blanket stitch (page 80). Follow the directions for the Chinese knot stitch (page 55) from Step 2, going down at **D**. Come up at **C** inside the previous stitch.

2. Repeat Step 1 to finish the row. To end the stitch, go down at **E**.

Variations: *Change the number or type of blanket stitches.*

Looped Petal Row

1. Follow Steps 1 and 2 for the blanket stitch looped (page 82). Work the first stitch angled slightly to the left. Work a second stitch straight up and a third stitch angled to the right.

2. Repeat Step 1 to finish the row. To end the stitch, go down at **F**.

Blanket Stitch Looped/Closed

1. Work 1 blanket stitch looped (page 82). Work 1 blanket stitch closed (page 84), going down at **F** and coming up at **G**.

2. Repeat Step 1 to finish the row. To end the stitch, go down at **H**.

Leaves and Stem Stalk or Row

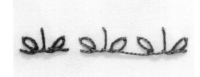

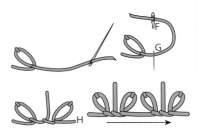

Stalk: Work 1 blanket stitch looped (page 82), angled to the left. Work 1 straight blanket stitch (page 80). Work 1 blanket stitch looped, angled to the right. To end the stitch, go down at **H**.

Row: Repeat the stalk a short distance away from the last stitch.

Blanket Stitch Stalk or Row

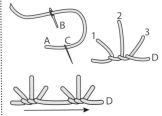

Stalk: Work 1 blanket stitch (page 80), angled to the left. Work 1 blanket stitch straight. Work 1 blanket stitch, angled to the right. To end the stitch, go down at **D**.

Row: Repeat from the pattern a short distance away from the last stitch.

Blanket and Stem Stitches

Blanket stitch   Blanket stitch looped

Blanket stitch up and down

Work 1 blanket stitch (page 80) and then 3 stem stitches (page 47). Repeat the pattern to finish the row.

Variations: *Change the type of blanket stitch or the number of stem stitches.*

Blanket and Scroll Stitches

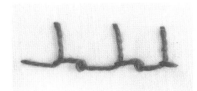

Blanket stitch   Blanket stitch closed

Blanket stitch angled

Work 1 blanket stitch (page 80) and 1 scroll stitch (page 53). Repeat the pattern to finish the row.

Variations: *Change the type of blanket stitch or the number of scroll stitches.*

Blanket and Chain Stitches

Blanket stitch straight with chain stitch

Blanket stitch grouped with chain stitch

1. Work 1 blanket stitch (page 80) or 1 set of grouped blanket stitches (page 80). Work 1 chain stitch (page 67), going down at **D** and up at **E**.

2. Repeat Step 1 to finish the row. To end the stitch, go down at **F** after a blanket stitch or chain stitch.

Blanket Stitches and Chain Stitch Open Tip

Blanket stitch up and down with chain stitch open tip

Blanket stitch closed with chain stitch open tip

1. Work 1 blanket stitch closed (page 84) or 1 set of blanket stitch up and down (page 81). Work 1 chain stitch open tip (page 68), going down at **D** and up at **E**.

2. Repeat Step 1 to finish the row. To end the stitch, go down at **F** after a blanket stitch or a chain stitch open tip.

Blanket and Chain Stitch Variations

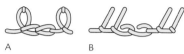

A   B

A. Follow the directions for the blanket and chain stitches (previous page), using a blanket stitch looped (page 82).

B. Follow the directions for the blanket and chain stitch open tip (previous page), using a grouped blanket stitched angled (page 82).

Blanket and Pistil Stitch Variations

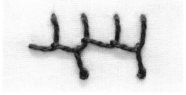

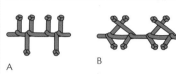

A   B

A. Follow the directions for the blanket stitch with knot tip (page 85) and blanket and pistil stitches (page 87).

B. Follow the directions for the blanket stitch with knot tip, using the blanket stitch crossed (page 84) directions and blanket and pistil stitches directions.

Blanket Stitch Netted

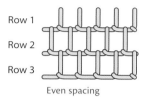

Row 1

Row 2

Row 3

Even spacing

1. Stitch 1 row of blanket stitches (page 80).

2. Stitch a second row below, with the tip of the stitch catching the bottom edge of the previous row.

Even, short, even spacing

Variations: *Change the length or type of the stitch, thread color, or number of rows.*

Blanket Stitch Feathered

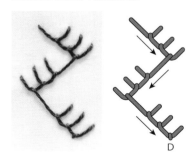

D

1. Work 1 blanket stitch (page 80), right-handed version, with a long beginning stitch. Work 2 more stitches.

2. Work 1 blanket stitch, left-handed version, with a long beginning stitch. Work 2 more stitches.

3. Repeat Steps 1 and 2 to finish the row. To end the stitch, go down at **D**.

Variations: *Change the length, spacing, or number of stitches in a pattern.*

Bell Flower Stitch

LEFT-HANDED

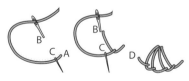

RIGHT-HANDED

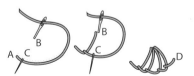

1. Draw a half-circle and mark the center. Follow Step 1 of the blanket stitch (page 80), *with B as the center point and A and C on the curved line.

2. Repeat from *, working the stitches around the curve. To end the stitch, go down at **D**.

Blanket Stitch Flower

LEFT-HANDED

First stitch

D
Last stitch

1. Draw a circle. Follow Step 1 of the blanket stitch (page 80), *with **B** as the tip of the stitch and **A** and **C** on the curved line.

2. Repeat from *, working the stitches around the circle. To end the stitch, go down next to the first stitch.

Note: *This stitch can be the base of the whip-stitch rose (page 57).*

RIGHT-HANDED

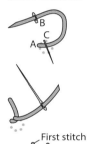

First stitch
Last stitch

Tree Stitch

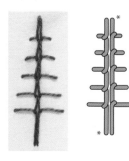

1. Stitch 1 row of blanket stitches (page 80), beginning the row at *. Vary the stitches from large to small. Turn the fabric.

2. Stitch a second row with the base close to the first row, beginning the row at *. Vary the stitches from small to large.

Buttonhole Circle Stitch

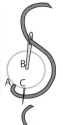

B
A C

For variations, draw an oval or a square shape.

1. Draw a circle and mark the center point. Follow Step 1 of the blanket stitch (page 80), *with **B** as the center of the stitch and **A** and **C** on the curved line.

2. Repeat from *, working the stitches around the circle. To end the stitch, go down next to the first stitch.

Boxed Star Stitch

B
A
C

1. Draw a box. Follow Step 1 of the blanket stitch with knot tip (page 85), *with **B** as the tip of the stitch and **A** and **C** on the drawn line.

2. Repeat from *, working the stitches around the square. To end the stitch, go down at next to **A**.

Blanket Stitch Closed Shapes

Triangle

Diamond

Pinwheel

Boat

Triangle: Follow the directions for the blanket stitch closed with details (page 85), with a short beginning and end stitch.

Diamond: Work 2 triangles.

Pinwheel: Draw a cross. Work 1 triangle on each spoke of the cross.

Boat: Work 1 triangle. Work 1 fly stitch (page 92).

Blanket Stitch Looped/Closed Shapes

Triangle

Box

Triangle angled

1   2
Bow

Triangle: Follow the directions for the blanket stitch looped/closed (page 87), with a short beginning and end stitch.

Box: Work 2 triangles, mirrored.

Triangle angled: Work 1 triangle with the loop angled.

Bow: Work 2 triangles angled.

Blanket Stitch Cobweb

1. Work 1 shell stitch (page 86).

2. Draw a line slightly above the curve of the previous row. Follow Step 1 of the blanket stitch (page 80), with **A** and **C** on the drawn line and **B** inside the stitch of the previous row. Work a second and third stitch. To end the stitch, go down at **D**.

Straight stitch

3. Repeat Steps 2 and 3 to finish the web.

4. Work a straight stitch (page 43) at the beginning of each row of stitches.

Pretty Butterfly Stitch

Wings: Follow the directions for the blanket stitch looped/closed (page 87), with a short beginning and end stitch. Work 1 more stitch opposite the first.

Antennae: Stitch 2 pistil stitches (page 44).

Legs: Stitch 2 straight stitches (page 43).

Sunrise Stitch

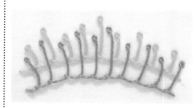

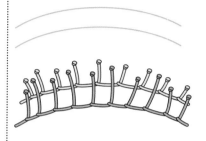

Draw 2 slightly curved rows. Stitch each row with the blanket stitch with knot tip (page 85).

- **Row 1:** Work the stitches close together at random heights.
- **Row 2:** Repeat, working the stitches with the tips grouped into the previous row.

Crossed Triangle Stitch

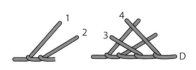

1. Following Steps 1 and 2 of the blanket stitch angled (page 82), work 2 stitches angled to the right to points 1 and 2.

2. Work 2 stitches angled to the left to points 3 and 4 crossing over the previous stitches. To end the stitch, go down at **D**.

Blanket Stitch Leaf

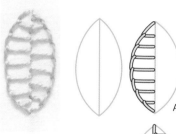

Draw a leaf shape. Follow Steps 1 and 2 of the blanket stitch (page 80), working a separate row for each half of the leaf.

A. Work the stitches with **A** and **C** of the stitch on the outer edge of the leaf and **B** on the inside line.

B. Work the stitches with **A** and **C** of the stitch on the inside line and **B** on the outside edge of the line.

FLY STITCHES

General Information

These individual stitches can be used as a single stitch, combined to create a border row, or added to another stitch to create a larger component.

Come up at point **A** and go down at point **B** in one motion. Come up at point **C**, which catches the loop formed by points **A** and **B**. The stitch would end with a point **D**. If the stitch has a detail, it would continue with point **E** and **F** stitches or more.

For a reference guide, use an erasable pen to draw the 3 beginning points of the stitch.

Fly Stitch

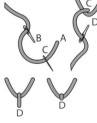

LEFT-HANDED

RIGHT-HANDED

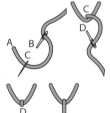

1. Come up at **A**. In one motion, go down at **B** and up at **C**. Wrap the working thread under the tip of the needle. Pull the needle through the fabric.

2. To end the stitch, go down at **D** or a short distance away for a long tail.

Fly Stitch Long Arm Straight or Angled

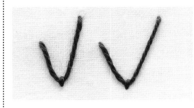

Straight: Follow the directions for the fly stitch (at left), with **B** higher than **A**.

Angled: Follow the directions for the fly stitch, with **B** higher than **A** and angled.

LEFT-HANDED

RIGHT-HANDED

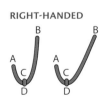

Fly Stitch Variations

Follow the directions for the fly stitch (at left), with or without tail.

A. Even cup: Points **A**, **B**, and **C** are equally spaced.

B. Short cup: Points **A** and **B** are further apart; point **C** is not as deep.

C. Long cup: Points **A** and **B** are closer together; point **C** is deeper.

Hourglass Stitch

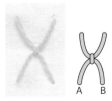

1. Work 1 fly stitch (above).

2. Come up at **A**; slide the needle under the end of the first stitch and go down at **B**.

Left-handed version: *In Step 2, reverse A for B and vice versa.*

Fly Stitch Offset

LEFT-HANDED

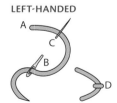

RIGHT-HANDED

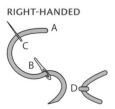

1. Come up at **A**. In one motion, go down at **B** and up at **C**. Wrap the working thread under the tip of the needle. Pull the needle through the fabric.

2. To end the stitch, go down at **D**.

Note: *B is lower and shorter than A. C can be to the middle or closer to one side of A or B.*

Fly Stitch with Straight Edge

LEFT-HANDED

RIGHT-HANDED

1. Come up at **A**. In one motion, go down at **B** and up at **C**. Wrap the working thread under the tip of the needle. Pull the needle through the fabric.

2. To end the stitch, go down at **D**.

Fly Stitch with Straight-Edge Variations

LEFT-HANDED

RIGHT-HANDED

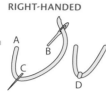

Follow the directions for the fly stitch with straight edge (at left).

- **Long straight edge: B** is lower than **A**.

- **Long arm: B** is higher than **A**.

Fly Stitch Soft Edges

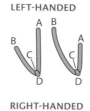

LEFT-HANDED

RIGHT-HANDED

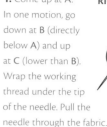

1. Come up at **A**. In one motion, go down at **B** (directly below **A**) and up at **C** (lower than **B**). Wrap the working thread under the tip of the needle. Pull the needle through the fabric.

2. To end the stitch, go down at **D**.

Fly Stitch Straight Edge Grouped

Side by side

Crossed

Follow the directions for the fly stitch with straight edge (above).

- **Side by side:** Work 1 stitch, left-handed version; work 1 stitch, right-handed version.

- **Crossed:** Work 1 stitch, right-handed version; work 1 stitch, left-handed version, crossing over the first stitch.

Fly Stitch with Pistil Stitch

Fly stitch

Fly stitch long arm

Fly stitch with straight edge

1. Follow Step 1 of the fly stitch (previous page). Point **C** now becomes point **A**.

2. Follow the directions for the pistil stitch (page 44), wrapping once. Go down at **D**.

LEFT-HANDED   **RIGHT-HANDED**

Fly Stitch with French Knot Stitch

LEFT-HANDED

RIGHT-HANDED

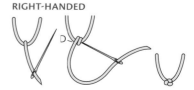

1. Follow Step 1 of the fly stitch (previous page). Point **C** now becomes point **A**.

2. Follow the directions for the French knot stitch (page 54), wrapping 1–3 times. Go down at **D**.

Fly Stitch with Loose Knot Stitch

LEFT-HANDED

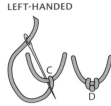

1. Follow Step 1 of the fly stitch (page 92). Go under the base stitch only; wrap the working thread under the tip of the needle. Pull the thread firmly around the base stitch.

RIGHT-HANDED

2. To end the stitch, go down at **D** or a short distance away.

Fly Stitch with Bullion Stitch Tail

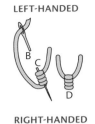

LEFT-HANDED

1. Come up at **A**. In one motion, go down at **B** and up at **C**, but do not pull the thread through the fabric. Wrap the thread around the needle 2 or 3 times. Pull the needle through the fabric.

RIGHT-HANDED

2. To end the stitch, go down at **D** just beyond the wraps.

Fern Stitch Modern

Straight stitch

Draw a line or follow a seam.

1. Work a straight stitch (page 43) on the line. *Work 1 fly stitch with a long tail (page 92); the tail is the beginning of the next stitch, with **D** on the line. *Note:* **A** and **B** are even with the top of the straight stitch; **C** and **D** are the same length as the straight stitch.

2. Repeat from * to finish the row.

Fly Stitch Twisted

Fly stitch

Fly stitch with long arm

1. Come up at **A**. In one motion, go down at **B** and up at **C**. Wrap the working thread over the needle and under the tip. Pull the needle through the fabric.

Fly stitch with straight edge

2. To end the stitch, go down at **D**.

Variations: Use a different fly stitch in Step 1.

LEFT-HANDED   **RIGHT-HANDED**

Fly Stitch with Lazy Daisy Stitch

Fly stitch

Fly stitch offset

1. Follow Step 1 of the fly stitch (page 92). In one motion, go down at **D** and up at **E**. Wrap the working thread under the tip of the needle. Pull the needle through the fabric.

Fly stitch with straight edge

2. To end the stitch, go down at **F**.

Variations: Use a different fly stitch in Step 1.

LEFT-HANDED   **RIGHT-HANDED**

Fly Stitch with Chain-Stitch Edge

Fly stitch

Fly stitch long arm

1. Follow Step 1 of the chain stitch (page 67). In one motion, go down at **D** and up at **E**. Wrap the working thread under the tip of the needle. Pull the needle through the fabric.

Fly stitch long arm straight edge

2. To end the stitch, go down at **F**.

Variations: Use a different fly stitch in Step 1.

LEFT-HANDED   **RIGHT-HANDED**

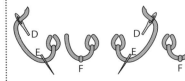

Fly Stitch Side by Side

LEFT-HANDED

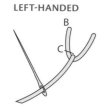

1. Follow Step 1 of the fly stitch (page 92), with **B** directly above **C**.

2. Work a second stitch, with **B** angled away from **C**. To end the stitch, go down at **D**.

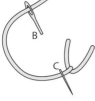

RIGHT-HANDED

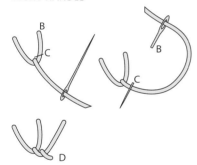

Magic Fly Stitch

LEFT-HANDED

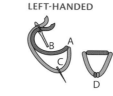

1. Thread the needle with 2 colors of the same thread. Knot the tails together.

2. Work 1 fly stitch (page 92), wrapping only one color of thread under the needle. As you pull the needle through the fabric, the second color will create a straight stitch from **A** to **B**.

3. To end the stitch, go down at **D**. Both threads will catch the end of the stitch.

RIGHT-HANDED

Fly Stitch Up and Down

LEFT-HANDED

1. Work 1 fly stitch (page 92). In one motion, go down at **D** and up at **E**. Loop the working thread over the tip of the needle.

2. Pull the needle through the fabric. Thread the needle under the loop and gently pull the thread to tighten. To end the stitch, go down at **F**.

RIGHT-HANDED

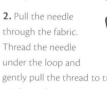

Fly Stitch Flowers

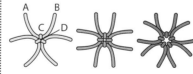

1. Choose a template (page 63) and draw in the lines.

2. Work the petals in the order they are shown. The line represents the center of each stitch and is a guide only.

- **Petal suggestions:** Fly stitch (page 92), fly stitch long arm (page 92), fly stitch twisted (previous page), fly stitch with French knot stitch (page 93) or another fly stitch

Optional: *Work a French knot stitch (page 54) or other knotted stitch in the center of the flower.*

Fly Stitch Flower Variations

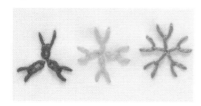

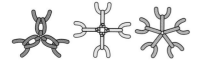

1. Choose a template (page 63) and draw in the lines.

2. Work the petals in the order they are shown, with the beginning and ending stitches higher than the line, the middle of the stitch at the tip of the line, and the end of the stitch in the center.

- **Petal suggestions:** Fly stitch with lazy daisy stitch (previous page), fly stitch with pistil stitch (page 93), or fly stitch with a long tail (page 92).

Optional: *Work a French knot stitch (page 54) or other knotted stitch in the center of the flower.*

Frilly Spiderweb Stitch

1. Work 1 fly stitch (page 92), elongated, for the center. Work 2 more stitches on either side of the first stitch.

2. Work straight stitches (page 43) down each stitch.

3. Work 1 straight stitch below the first row, connecting the adjacent sides of each fly stitch. Work a second row below the first.

Skeleton Leaf Stitch

 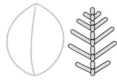

1. Draw a leaf shape.

2. Follow the directions for the fern stitch modern (page 94), working the tips of the stitch along the drawn outer edges and the center of the stitch down the middle line.

Agapanthus Stitch

1. Draw the line for the stem; stitch with the stem stitch (page 47).

2. Draw the lines for the petals; stitch with either the fly stitch with long tail (page 92) or with the straight stitch (page 43).

Wisteria Stitch

1. Draw in the line for the stem; stitch with the stem stitch (page 47).

2. Beginning at the end of the stem, stitch a fly stitch (page 92). Work additional stitches above and around the previous stitch.

3. Stitch 2 lazy daisy stitches (page 60) for the leaves.

Fly Stitch Mirrored

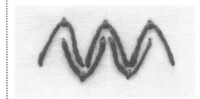

1. Stitch a row of fly stitches (page 92), beginning the row at *. Turn the fabric.

2. Stitch a second row, with the spokes worked next to the first row, beginning the row at *.

Variations:
Change the length or type of the stitch, or where the stitches meet.

Fly stitch long arm

Fly stitch straight edge

Triangle Stitch

1. Follow the directions for the fly stitch offset (page 92), right-handed version, with **A** above **B** and **C** even with **B**.

2. Work a second stitch left-handed, stitching into points **A** and **B** of the previous stitch.

Heart Stitch

1. Follow the directions for the fly stitch offset (page 92), right-handed version, with **A** above **B** and **C** higher than **A**.

2. Work a second stitch, left-handed version, stitching into points **A** and **B** of the previous stitch.

Fly Stitch Stacked and Variations

Stacked

Fly stitch with lazy daisy stitch

Fly stitch with French knot stitch

Fly stitch long arm

Variation

Work 1 fly stitch (page 92). Work the next 2 stitches below and around the previous stitch.

Variations: *Work the stitch in different colors or substitute a different fly stitch.*

Fly Stitch Long Arm Crossed Group or Row

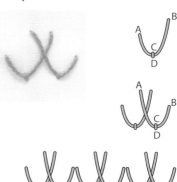

Group: Work 1 fly stitch long arm angled (page 92), right-handed version. Work a second stitch, left-handed version, crossing over the previous stitch.

Row: Repeat Step 1 across a seam or line.

Fly Stitch Reversed

2nd
1st

Fly stitch wider

Fly stitch with tail

Fly stitch with French knot stitch

Work 1 fly stitch (page 92). Work the second stitch upside down and crossing over the first.

Variations: *Work the second stitch in a different color or substitute a different fly stitch.*

Fly Stitch Double

1st
2nd

Fly stitch long and short

Fly stitch with straight edge

Fly stitch with French knot stitch

Work 1 fly stitch (page 92) wide and short. Work the second stitch longer, with the tips inside and crossing over the first stitch.

Variations: *Work the stitches in a different color or substitute a different fly stitch.*

Fly Stitch Capped

E F E F

Fly stitch with longer body

Fly stitch long arm

Fly stitch straight edge

1. Follow the directions for the fly stitch (page 92).

2. Work a straight stitch (page 43) from **E** to **F** on each tip of the stitch.

Left-handed version: *In Step 2, reverse **E** for **F** and vice versa.*

Variations: *Use a different color of thread for the cap stitch.*

Crown Stitch

Work 1 fly stitch with a long tail (page 92). Work 2 straight stitches (page 43) from **A** to **B**.

Fly Stitch Mock Chevron

1. Work a row of fly stitches (page 92).

2. Work a straight stitch (page 43) over each tip.

Variations: *Change the length or type of the stitch.*

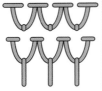

Fly stitch with long tail

Fly stitch long arm group

Fly Stitch Plaited

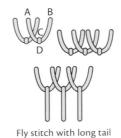

Fly stitch with long tail

Fly stitch with French knot stitch

1. Work 1 fly stitch (page 92). *Begin the next stitch inside the previous stitch.

2. Repeat from * to complete the row

Variations: *Change the length or type of the stitch.*

Fly Stitch Netted

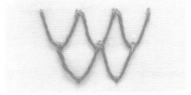

1st
2nd

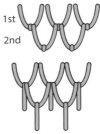

Fly stitch with long tail

Fly stitch with lazy daisy stitch

1. Stitch 1 row of fly stitches (page 92).

2. Stitch a second row below, with the tips of the stitch worked into the 2 adjacent stitches above it.

Variations: *Change the length or type of the stitch, or the color of the thread in the second row.*

Fishhook Stitch

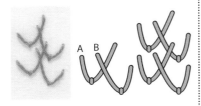

1. Work 1 fly stitch long arm (page 92), angled right-handed version.

2. Work the next stitch, left-handed version, with point **B** of the stitch even with point **A** of the previous stitch.

3. To finish the row, repeat Steps 1 and 2, working the next group of stitches below the previous group.

Fly Stitch Chain Link

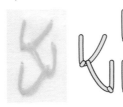

1. Work 1 fly stitch with straight edge (page 93), right-handed version.

2. Work the next stitch, left-handed version, with point **B** worked into the previous stitch.

3. Repeat Steps 1 and 2 to finish the row, working the stitches below and into the previous stitch.

Fly Stitch Fancy Link

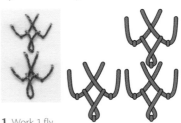

1. Work 1 fly stitch long arm crossed group (page 97).

2. Work 1 fly stitch twisted (page 94), with the tips of the stitch worked into the 2 stitches above it.

3. To finish the row, repeat Steps 1 and 2. End the row with either stitch.

FEATHER STITCHES

General Information

These continuous stitches can be used for a border row or to create a shape. After the stitch is formed, individual stitches can be added to the tips or around the base to create a larger design.

The following stitches are formed by coming up at point **A** and then, in one motion, going down at point **B** and coming up at point **C**, which catches the loop formed by points **A** and **B**. Point **C** becomes point **A** for the following stitch. The stitch is work continuously and would end at point **D**. If the stitch has a detail, it would continue with point **E** and **F** stitches or more.

FEATHER STITCH SPACING GUIDES

The basic feather stitches can be made easier if you first practice with this grid method. With an erasable pen, draw 2 or more vertical parallel lines the length and width of the row; then mark the same spacing horizontally. Number the vertical lines as shown. Refer to the basic feather stitch instructions (page 100).

Left-handed version: *List the numbering on the vertical lines from right to left and reverse points A and B.*

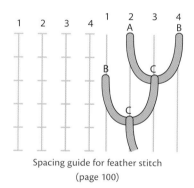

Spacing guide for feather stitch
(page 100)

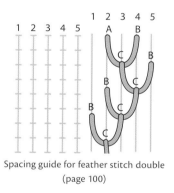

Spacing guide for feather stitch double
(page 100)

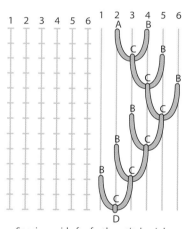

Spacing guide for feather stitch triple
(page 100)

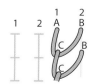

Spacing guide for feather stitch single
(page 102)

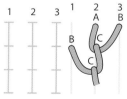

Spacing guide for feather stitch
straight center (page 102)

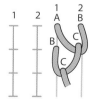

Spacing guide for feather stitch
straight side (page 102) or
feather stitch closed (page 102)

Feather Stitch

Even spaced

Wide and short

Narrow and long

The feather stitch can vary dramatically by changing the distance between points **A**, **B**, and **C**.

Work this stitch between 4 vertical lines.

1. Come up at **A**. *In one motion, go down at **B** and up at **C**. Wrap the working thread under the tip of the needle. Pull the needle through the fabric.

2. Repeat from *, working the next stitch below and in the opposite direction.

3. Repeat Steps 1 and 2 to finish the row. To end the stitch, go down at **D**.

LEFT-HANDED

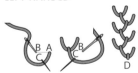

RIGHT-HANDED

Magic Feather Stitch

LEFT-HANDED

1. Thread the needle with 2 colors of the same thread. Knot the tails together.

2. Come up at **A**. *In one motion, go down at **B** and up at **C**; wrap one color of thread only under the needle. As you pull the needle through the fabric, the second color will create a straight stitch from **A** to **B**.

RIGHT-HANDED

3. Repeat from * to finish the row, working the next stitch below and in the opposite direction, altering the thread color.

4. To end the stitch, go down at **D**; both threads will catch the end of the stitch.

Feather Stitch Double

LEFT-HANDED

RIGHT-HANDED

Work this stitch between 5 vertical lines.

1. Follow Step 1 of the feather stitch (at left). Work a second stitch below and in the same direction.

2. Follow Step 2 of the feather stitch. Work a second stitch below and in the same direction.

3. Repeat Steps 1 and 2 to finish the row. To end the stitch, go down at **D**.

Feather Stitch Triple

Work this stitch between 6 vertical lines.

1. Follow Step 1 of the feather stitch (above). Work a second and third stitch below and in the same direction.

2. Follow Step 2 of the feather stitch. Work a second and third stitch below and in the same direction.

3. Repeat Steps 1 and 2 to finish the row. To end the stitch, go down at **D**.

LEFT-HANDED

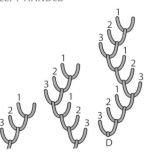

RIGHT-HANDED

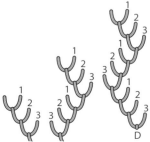

Feather Stitch Long Arm

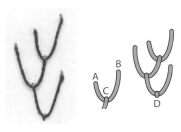

1. Follow Steps 1 and 2 of the feather stitch (previous page), with **B** higher than **A**.

2. Repeat Step 1 to finish the row. To end the stitch, go down at **D**.

Feather Stitch Short Arm

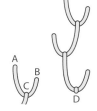

1. Follow Steps 1 and 2 of the feather stitch (previous page), with **B** lower than **A**.

2. Repeat Step 1 to finish the row. To end the stitch, go down at **D**.

Feather Stitch Elongated

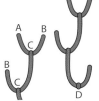

1. Follow Step 1 of the feather stitch (previous page).

2. Follow Step 2, with a space between **C** of the previous stitch and **B** of the new stitch.

3. Repeat Steps 1 and 2 to finish the row, leaving a long space between the previous and next stitch. To end the stitch, go down at **D**.

Feather Stitch Piggyback

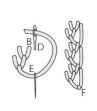

Work this stitch between 4 vertical lines.

1. Follow Steps 1 and 2 of the feather stitch (previous page), working the stitches to the left.

2. In one motion, go down at **D** (parallel to **B** of the first stitch) and up at **E** (below the second stitch), working the stitch to the right. Wrap the working thread under the tip of the needle. Pull the needle through the fabric.

3. Repeat Steps 1 and 2 to finish the row. To end the stitch, go down at **F**.

Left-handed version: In Step 1, work the stitches to the right. In Step 2, work the stitch to the left.

Feather Stitch Double Variations

Follow the directions for the feather stitch double (previous page), changing the length and width of the stitches.

In the second stitch, point **B** is parallel with **B** of the first stitch, making the second stitch longer than the first.

In the second stitch, point **B** is longer and **C** shorter than the first stitch, making the second stitch angled.

Feather Stitch Triple Variations

Follow the directions for the feather stitch triple (previous page), changing the length and width of the stitches.

The second and third stitches decrease in size from the first stitch.

The second and third stitches increase in size from the first stitch.

Feather Stitch Closed

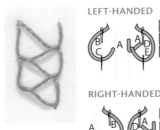

LEFT-HANDED

RIGHT-HANDED

Work this stitch between 2 vertical lines.

1. Follow Step 1 of the feather stitch (page 100), with **A** on one line and **B** and **C** on the other line.

2. Follow Step 2 of the feather stitch, with **D** close to **A** of the previous stitch and both **D** and **E** on the same line.

3. Repeat Steps 1 and 2 to finish the row. To end the stitch, go down at **F**.

Feather Stitch Single

LEFT-HANDED

Work this stitch between 2 vertical lines.

RIGHT-HANDED

1. Come up at **A**. Follow Step 1 of the feather stitch (page 100) from *, with **B** directly across from **A**, and **A** and **C** on the line.

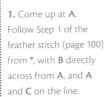

2. Repeat from * to finish the row. To end the stitch, go down at **D**.

Feather Stitch Straight Center

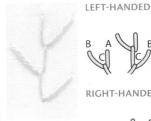

LEFT-HANDED

RIGHT-HANDED

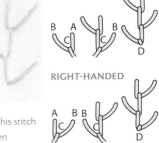

Work this stitch between 3 vertical lines.

1. Come up at **A**. Follow Step 1 of the feather stitch (page 100) from *, with **A** and **C** on the middle line and **B** on an outer line.

2. Repeat Step 1 from * to finish the row, working the next stitch below and in the opposite direction. To end the stitch, go down at **D**.

Feather Stitch Straight Side

LEFT-HANDED

RIGHT-HANDED

Work this stitch between 2 vertical lines.

1. Come up at **A**. Follow Step 1 of the feather stitch (page 100) from *, with **A** on one line and **B** and **C** on the other line.

2. Repeat Step 1 from * to finish the row, working the next stitch below and in the opposite direction. To end the stitch, go down at **D**.

Feather Stitch Variations

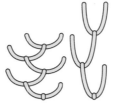

Feather stitch (page 100)

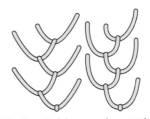

Feather stitch long arm (page 101)

Feather stitch elongated (page 101)

Feather stitch single (above center)

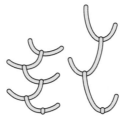

Feather stitch short arm (page 101)

Follow the directions for the feather stitch listed, changing the length and width of the stitches.

Feather Stitch Mirrored

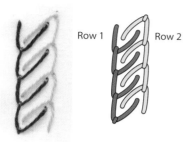

Row 1   Row 2

Row 1: Stitch 1 row of feather stitch single (previous page).

Row 2: Turn the fabric. Stitch a second row, with the tips worked into the previous row.

Variations: *Change the spacing of the stitches or use a second color of thread for row 2.*

Feather Stitch Straight Center Variations

With feather stitch double (page 100)

Follow the directions for the feather stitch straight center (previous page), using these stitch variations (above).

With feather stitch long arm (page 101)

Feather Stitch Straight Side Variations

With feather stitch straight side alternating short and long stitches

Follow the directions for the feather stitch straight side (previous page), using these stitch variations (above).

With feather stitch double (page 100)

Feather Stitch Overlaid

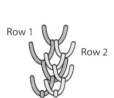

Row 1   Row 2

Row 1: Stitch 1 row of feather stitches (page 100).

Row 2: Stitch a second row, overlapping the stitches of the previous row.

Variations: *Change the type of feather stitch or use a second color of thread for row 2.*

Maidenhair Fern Stitch

LEFT-HANDED

RIGHT-HANDED

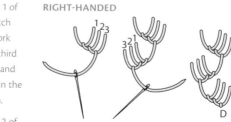

1. Follow Step 1 of the feather stitch (page 100). Work a second and third stitch close to and slightly below in the same direction.

2. Follow Step 2 of the feather stitch. Work a second and third stitch close to and slightly below in the same direction.

3. Repeat Steps 1 and 2 to finish the row. To end the stitch, go down at **D**.

Maidenhair Fern Stitch Single

LEFT-HANDED

1. Follow Step 1 of the maidenhair fern stitch (page 103).

RIGHT-HANDED

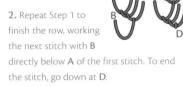

2. Repeat Step 1 to finish the row, working the next stitch with **B** directly below **A** of the first stitch. To end the stitch, go down at **D**.

Feather Stitch Double Cup

LEFT-HANDED

1. Follow Step 1 of the feather stitch (page 100), with a longer width and shorter length. *In one motion, go down at **D** and up at **E**; **E** now becomes **A** for the following stitch

2. Follow Step 2 of the feather stitch, with a longer width and shorter length. Follow Step 1 from *.

3. Repeat Steps 1 and 2 to finish the row. To end the stitch, go down at **F**.

RIGHT-HANDED

Feather Stitch Cobwebbed

LEFT-HANDED

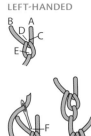

1. Follow Step 1 of the feather stitch straight center (page 102). *Work a chain stitch (page 67) from **D** to **E** inside the loop, below the feather stitch and on the line. Work a second chain stitch from **F** to **G**, wider and below the first.

2. Follow Step 2 of the feather stitch straight center. Follow Step 1 from *.

RIGHT-HANDED

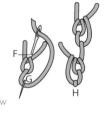

3. Repeat Steps 1 and 2 to finish the row. To end the stitch, go down at **H**.

Fishnet Stitch

First row: Follow Step 1 of the feather stitch double (page 100). Go down at **D** to end the row.

Second row: Follow Step 1 of the feather stitch triple (page 100), working the stitches into the previous row. Go down at **D** to end the row. Repeat this step to almost the end of the section that you are working on.

Last row: Follow Step 1 of the feather stitch double, working the stitch into the previous row. Go down at **D** to end the row.

LEFT-HANDED

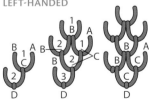

RIGHT-HANDED

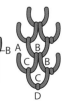

Feather Stitch Twisted

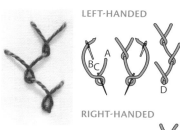

LEFT-HANDED

RIGHT-HANDED

Work this stitch between 4 vertical rows.

1. Come up at **A**. *In one motion, go down at **B** and up at **C**. Wrap the working thread over the needle and under the tip. Pull the needle through the fabric.

2. Repeat Step 1 from *, working the next stitch below and in the opposite direction.

3. Repeat Steps 1 and 2 to finish the row. To end the stitch, go down at **D**.

Feather Stitch Looped

LEFT-HANDED

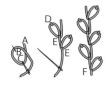

RIGHT-HANDED

Work this stitch between 4 vertical rows.

1. Come up at **A**. *In one motion, go down at **B** and up at **C**. Wrap the working thread under the eye and the tip of the needle and back to the base of the stitch. Pull the needle through the fabric. Go down at **D** to catch the loop. Come up at **E**.

2. Repeat Step 1 from *, working the next stitch below and in the opposite direction. To end the stitch, go down at **F**.

Feather Stitch Twisted Loop

LEFT-HANDED

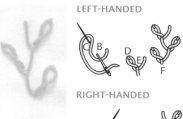

RIGHT-HANDED

Work this stitch between 4 vertical rows.

1. Come up at **A**. *In one motion, go down at **B** and up at **C** (angled away). Wrap the working thread under the eye of the needle, over and then under the tip of the needle, and back to the base. Pull the needle through the fabric. Go down at **D** to catch the loop. Come up at **E**.

2. Repeat Step 1 from *, working the next stitch below and in the opposite direction. To end the stitch, go down at **F**.

Feather Stitch Random or Organic

Follow the directions for the feather stitch double or triple (page 100), working the stitches in a variety of groups or varying the stitch lengths.

Feather Stitch with Lazy Daisy Stitch Detail

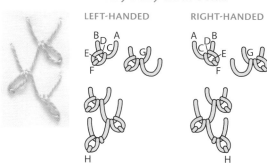

LEFT-HANDED   **RIGHT-HANDED**

1. Work 1 feather stitch (page 100). Follow Steps 1 and 2 of the lazy daisy stitch (page 60): **C**, **D**, **E**, and **F**. Come up at **G**.

2. Repeat Step 1, working the next stitch below and in the opposite direction. To end the stitch, go down at **H**.

Feather Stitch with Bell Flower Stitch

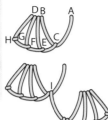

1. Work 1 feather stitch (page 100).

2. In one motion, go down at **D** and up at **E**, long and slightly angled to the side. Work a second stitch: **D** and **F**, and third stitch: **D** and **G**, slightly higher than the first and decreasing in size. Go down at **H**.

3. Repeat Steps 1 and 2 to finish the row, working the next group of stitches below and in the opposite direction. To end the stitch, go down at **J**.

RIGHT-HANDED

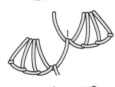

Feather Stitch with Chain-Stitch Edge

LEFT-HANDED

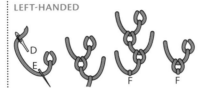

RIGHT-HANDED

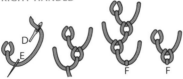

Work this stitch between 4 vertical rows.

1. Work 1 chain stitch (page 67).

2. Follow Step 1 of the feather stitch (page 100) from *. **D** and **E** replace **B** and **C** in the directions.

3. Repeat Steps 1 and 2 to finish the row, working the next group of stitches below and in the opposite direction. To end the stitch, go down at **F**, after the feather or a chain stitch.

Feather Stitch with Chain-Stitch Center

LEFT-HANDED

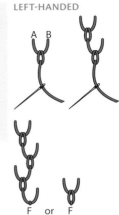

1. Work 1 feather stitch (page 100). Work a chain stitch (page 67) inside the loop and below the feather stitch.

2. Repeat Step 1 to finish the row, working the next group of stitches below and in the opposite direction. To end the stitch, go down at **F**, after the feather or a chain stitch.

RIGHT-HANDED

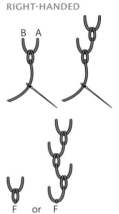

Feather Stitch with Knot Tip

LEFT-HANDED

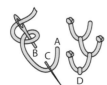

RIGHT-HANDED

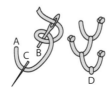

1. Come up at **A**. *Loop the thread over your finger and place the loop next to the fabric. Backstitch the needle in one motion down at an angle at **B** through the loop and up at **C**. Pull the thread tightly; then pull the needle through the fabric.

2. Follow Step 1 from * to finish the row, working the next stitch below and in the opposite direction. To end the stitch, go down at **D**.

Feather Stitch with Loose Knot Stitch

LEFT-HANDED

RIGHT-HANDED

1. Work 1 feather stitch (page 100). Go under the base stitch only; wrap the working thread under the tip of the needle. Pull the thread firmly around the base stitch.

2. Repeat Step 1 to finish the row, working the next stitch below and in the opposite direction. To end the stitch, go down at **D**.

Feather Stitch with Outline Stitches

Feather stitch (page 100)

Feather stitch single (page 102)

Feather stitch double (page 100)

Follow the directions for the feather stitch or variations listed, working 3 outline (page 47) or stem stitches (page 47) between the feather stitches. Repeat the pattern to the end of the row.

Feather and Blanket Stitches

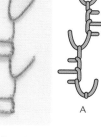

A

B

C

A. Follow the directions for the feather stitch (page 100) with blanket stitch height variations (page 80).

B. Follow the directions for the feather stitch double (page 100) with blanket stitch grouped (page 80) worked at an angle.

C. Follow the directions for the feather stitch straight center (page 102) with blanket stitch grouped.

Feather and Chain Stitches

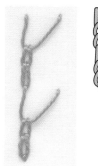

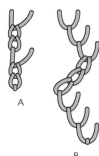

A

B

C

A. Follow the directions for the feather stitch single (page 102) with 2 chain stitches (page 67).

B. Follow the directions for the feather stitch triple (page 100) with 3 chain stitches worked at an angle.

C. Follow the directions for the feather stitch straight side (page 102) with 2 chain stitches.

Variations: *Substitute a different chain stitch.*

Feather and Looped Stitches

A

B

C

A. Follow the directions for the chain stitch (page 67) with feather stitch looped (page 105).

B. Follow the directions for the feather stitch looped with feather stitch triple (page 100).

C. Follow the directions for the feather stitch looped with feather stitch straight center (page 102).

Feather Stitch Up and Down

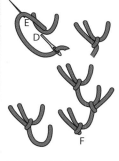

LEFT-HANDED

F

RIGHT-HANDED

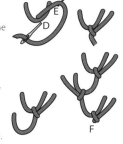

F

1. Work 1 feather stitch (page 100). In one motion, go down at **D** and up at **E**. Loop the working thread over the tip of the needle. Pull the needle through the fabric. Pass the needle under the loop and gently pull the thread to tighten.

2. Repeat Step 1, working the next group of stitches below and in the opposite direction. To end the stitch, go down at **F**.

Feather Stitch Up and Down Variation

LEFT-HANDED

RIGHT-HANDED

1. Follow Step 1 of the feather stitch up and down (page 107). Work a second up-and-down stitch at **F** and **G**.

2. Repeat Step 1 to finish the row, working the next group of stitches below and in the opposite direction. To end the stitch, go down at **H** under the bar at **F**.

Feather Stitch with Sheaf Stitch Edge

LEFT-HANDED

RIGHT-HANDED

1. Follow Step 1 of the maidenhair fern stitch (page 103); go down at **D**. Follow Steps 2 and 3 of the sheaf stitch (page 44). Come up at **E**.

2. Repeat Step 1 to finish the row, working the next group of stitches below and in the opposite direction.

Feather Stitch with Fly Stitch Detail

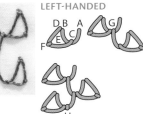

LEFT-HANDED

RIGHT-HANDED

1. *Work 1 feather stitch (page 100). Work 1 fly stitch (page 92): **C, D, E,** and **F**. Come up at **G**.

2. Repeat from *, working the next group of stitches below and in the opposite direction.

To end the stitch, go down at **H**.

Feather Stitch Looped Variations

Follow the directions for any of these stitches, working the feather stitch looped (page 105) for the tip.

Feather stitch double (page 100)

Feather stitch short arm (page 101)

Feather stitch straight side (page 102)

Feather Stitch Twisted Loop Variations

Follow the directions for any of these stitches, working the feather stitch twisted loop (page 105) for the tip.

Feather stitch elongated (page 101)

Feather stitch single (page 102)

Feather stitch triple (page 100)

Feather Stitch with Lazy Daisy Stitch Detail Variations

Feather stitch single
(page 102)

Feather stitch
double (page 100)

Feather stitch
straight side
(page 102)

Follow the directions for the feather stitch with lazy daisy stitch detail (page 105), using the suggested variations.

Feather Stitch Vines

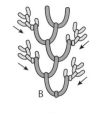

B

Vine A

C

Vine A: Stitch 1 row of feather stitches (page 100). **Branches:** Stitch a row of stem stitches (page 47) from a tip in the vine.

Vine B: Stitch 1 row of feather stitches. **Branches:** Stitch a short row of feather stitches onto the tip in the vine.

Vine C: Stitch 1 row of feather stitches organic (page 105). **Branches:** Stitch a row of chain stitches (page 67) from a tip in the vine.

Feather Stitch with Fly Stitch Detail Variations

Feather stitch single
(page 102)

Feather stitch
straight center
(page 102)

Feather stitch
double (page 100)

Follow the directions for the feather stitch with fly stitch detail (page 108) using the suggested variations above.

Feather Stitch with Chain-Stitch Edge or Center Variations

Feather stitch
single (page 102)

Feather stitch
straight center
(page 102)

Feather stitch closed
(page 102)

Follow the directions for the feather stitch with chain-stitch edge (page 106) using the suggested variations.

Follow the directions for the feather stitch with chain-stitch center (page 106) using the suggested variations.

Feather stitch (page 100) with the chain stitch angled

Feather stitch single
(page 102) with a
small chain stitch

Feather stitch
double variation
(page 101)

FEATHER STITCHES

FLEET STITCHES

General Information

These individual stitches can be used as a single stitch, combined to create a border row, or added to another stitch to create a larger component.

The following stitches are formed by coming up at point **A** and then, in one motion, going down at point **B** and coming up at point **C**, which catches the loop formed by points **A** and **B**. The stitch would end with a point **D**. If the stitch has a detail, it would continue with point **E** and **F** stitches or more.

For reference, use an erasable pen to draw the 3 beginning points of the stitch.

Fleet Stitch

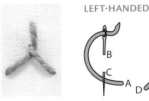

1. Come up at **A**. In one motion, go down at **B** and up at **C**. Wrap the working thread under the tip of the needle. Pull the needle through the fabric.

2. To end the stitch, go down at **D**.

Fleet Stitch Long Arm

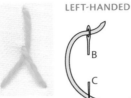

1. Follow the directions for the fleet stitch (at left), with point **B** higher and points **A** and **D** closer together.

Fleet Stitch with Arrow Tip Detail

1. Work 1 fleet stitch (at left).

2. Work 2 straight stitches (page 43) from **E** to **F**.

Steeple and Cross Stitch

1. Work 1 fleet stitch (above).

2. Work 1 straight stitch (page 43) from **E** to **F**.

Fleet Stitch with Angled Arm

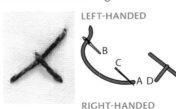

1. Come up at **A**. In one motion, go down at **B** and up at **C**, angling back toward **A**. Wrap the working thread under the tip of the needle. Pull the needle through the fabric.

2. To end the stitch, go down at **D**, which is below **B**.

Fleet Stitch Offset

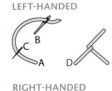

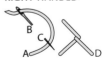

1. Come up at **A**. In one motion, go down at **B** (above **A** and angled away) and up at **C**. Wrap the working thread under the tip of the needle. Pull the needle through the fabric.

2. To end the stitch, go down at **D**.

Fleet Stitch with Loose Knot Stitch

LEFT-HANDED

RIGHT-HANDED

1. Follow Step 1 of the fleet stitch (page 110). Go under the base stitch only; wrap the working thread under the tip of the needle. Pull the thread firmly around the base stitch.

2. To end the stitch, go down at **D**.

Fleet Stitch with Lazy Daisy Stitch

LEFT-HANDED

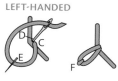

RIGHT-HANDED

1. Follow Step 1 of the fleet stitch (page 110).

In one motion, go down at **D** and up at **E**. Wrap the working thread under the tip of the needle. Pull the needle through the fabric.

2. To end the stitch, go down at **F**.

Fleet Stitch with Knot Tip

LEFT-HANDED

RIGHT-HANDED

1. Come up at **A**. Loop the thread over your finger and place the loop next to the fabric. Backstitch the needle in one motion down at an angle at **B** through the loop and up at **C**. Pull the thread tightly; then pull the needle through the fabric.

2. To finish the stitch, go down at **D**.

Fleet Stitch with Pistil Stitch

LEFT-HANDED

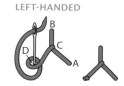

RIGHT-HANDED

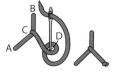

1. Follow Step 1 of the fleet stitch (page 110).

2. Follow the directions for the Chinese knot stitch (page 55) from Step 2, going down at **D**.

Fleet Stitch Reversed

Work 1 fleet stitch (page 110). Work a second stitch upside down and crossing over the first.

Variations: *Work the second stitch in a different color or substitute a different fly stitch.*

Fleet Stitches Crossed

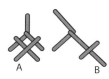

A. Work 1 fleet stitch (page 110). Work 1 cross stitch (page 122) across the bottom portion of the stitch.

B. Work 1 fleet stitch offset (page 110). Work 1 straight stitch (page 43) across the leg of the stitch.

Fleet Stitch Row

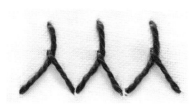

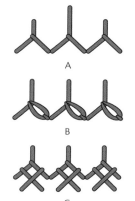

Work a row of fleet stitches (page 110) or other fleet stitch across a line or seam.

A. Fleet stitch and fleet stitch long arm (page 110)

B. Fleet stitch with lazy daisy stitch (page 111)

C. Fleet stitch crossed variation A (above right).

Fleet Stitch Looped

LEFT-HANDED

RIGHT-HANDED

1. Come up at **A**. In one motion, go down at **B** and up at **C**. Wrap the working thread under the eye and the tip of the needle and back to the base of the stitch. Pull the needle through the fabric. Go down at **D**.

2. To finish the stitch, come up at **E** and go down at **F**.

Fleet Stitch Twisted Loop

LEFT-HANDED

RIGHT-HANDED

1. Come up at **A**. In one motion, go down at **B** and up at **C**. Wrap the working thread under the eye of the needle and then over and under the tip of the needle.

2. Pull the needle through the fabric. Go down at **D**. To finish the stitch, come up at **E** and go down at **F**.

Fleet Stitch Twisted with French Knot

LEFT-HANDED

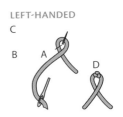

RIGHT-HANDED

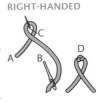

1. Come up at **A**. In one motion, go down at **B** and up at **C**. Wrap the working thread over the needle and under the tip. Pull the needle through the fabric.

2. Work a 2-wrap French knot (page 54); go down at **D**.

Fleet Stitch Up and Down

LEFT-HANDED

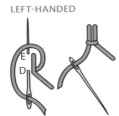

RIGHT-HANDED

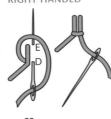

1. Follow Step 1 of the fleet stitch (page 110). In one motion, go down at **D** and up at **E**. Loop the working thread over the tip of the needle.

2. Pull the needle through the fabric. Thread the needle under the loop and gently pull the thread to tighten. To end the stitch, go down at **F**.

Fleet Stitch Flowers

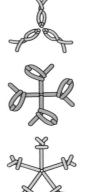

1. Choose a template (page 63) and draw in the lines.

2. Work the petals in the order they are shown. The line represents the center of each stitch and is a guide only.

• **Petal suggestions:** Fleet stitch twisted with French knot (page 112), fleet stitch with lazy daisy stitch (page 111), or steeple and cross stitch (page 110)

Optional: *Work a French knot stitch (page 54) or other knotted stitch in the center of the flower.*

Snowflake Stitch

1. Draw in the lines of the template.

2. Stitch each line with the fleet stitch (page 110), with points **A** and **D** higher than the line, point **B** at the center, and point **C** at the tip of the line.

3. Stitch a 2-wrap French knot (page 54) in the center. Stitch a 1-wrap French knot stitch between each fleet stitch.

Fleet Stitch Plaited

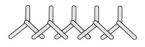

1. Work 1 fleet stitch (page 110), steeple and cross stitches (page 110), or another fleet stitch.

2. Begin the next stitch inside the previous stitch. Repeat this step across the row.

Fleet Stitch Offset Row Plaited

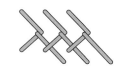

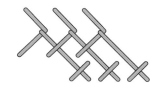

1. Work 1 fleet stitch offset (page 110) or fleet stitch crossed offset (page 111).

2. Begin the next stitch inside the previous stitch. Repeat this step across the row.

Fleet Stitch Netted

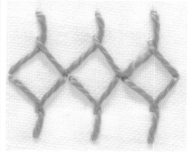

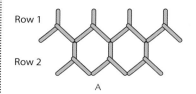

Row 1

Row 2

A

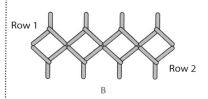

Row 1

Row 2

B

Stitch 1 row of fleet stitches (page 110). Then follow one of the directions below.

A. Stitch a second row below, with **B** of the stitch worked between **D** and **A** of the stitches in the previous row.

B. Turn the fabric. Stitch a second row of stitches below, with **A** next to **D** of the first stitch and **D** next to **A** of the first stitch.

Variations: *Change the length or type of the stitch, or color of the thread in the second row.*

CRETAN STITCHES

General Information

These continuous stitches can be used for a border row or to create a shape. After the stitch is formed, individual stitches can be added to the tips or around the base to create a larger design.

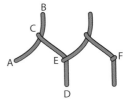

The following stitches are formed by coming up at point **A** and then, in one motion, going down at point **B** and coming up at point **C**, which catches the loop formed by points **A** and **B**. The stitch continues by going down at point **D** and coming up at point **E**. Point **E** becomes point **A** for the following stitch. The stitch is work continuously and would end at point **F**. If the stitch has a detail, it would continue with point **G** and **H** stitches or more.

CRETAN STITCH SPACING GUIDES

The basic cretan stitches can be made easier if you first practice with this grid method. Draw 3 or more horizontal parallel lines the length and width of the row with an erasable pen; then mark the same spacing vertically. Number the horizontal lines as shown. Refer to the basic cretan stitch instructions (below).

Left-handed version: *The numbering on the horizontal lines should be listed on the right-hand side. The points on the example of the stitch would then be reversed.*

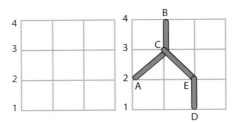

Spacing guide cretan stitch 4-row

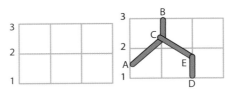

Spacing guide cretan stitch 3-row

Cretan Stitch 4-Row

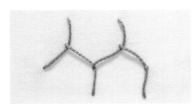

LEFT-HANDED

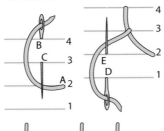

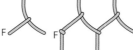

RIGHT-HANDED

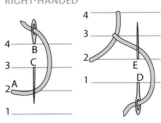

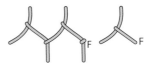

Work this stitch between 4 horizontal rows.

1. Come up at **A** on line 2. *In one motion, go down at **B** on line 4 and up at **C** on line 3. Wrap the working thread under the tip of the needle. Pull the needle through the fabric.

2. In one motion, go down at **D** on line 1 and up at **E** on line 2. Wrap the working thread under the tip of the needle. Pull the needle through the fabric.

3. Repeat from * to finish the row. To end the stitch, go down at **F**, either after Step 1 or Step 2.

Cretan Stitch 3-Row

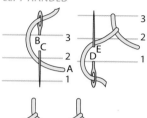

LEFT-HANDED

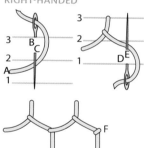

RIGHT-HANDED

1. Come up at **A** slightly below line 2. *In one motion, go down at **B** on line 3 and up at **C** slightly above line 2. Wrap the working thread under the tip of the needle. Pull the needle through the fabric.

2. In one motion, go down at **D** on line 1 and up at **E** slightly below line 2. Wrap the working thread under the tip of the needle. Pull the needle through the fabric.

3. Repeat from * to finish the row. To end the stitch, go down at **F**, either after Step 1 or Step 2.

Cretan Stitch Angled 4-Row

LEFT-HANDED

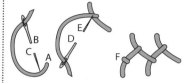

RIGHT-HANDED

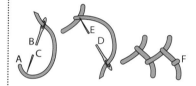

1. Come up at **A**. Follow Step 1 of the cretan stitch 4-row (page 114) from *, with **B** and **C** angled back toward **A**.

2. Follow Step 2 with **D** and **E** angled back toward **C** of the previous stitch.

3. Repeat from * to finish the row. To end the stitch, go down at **F**, either after Step 1 or Step 2.

Cretan Stitch Angled 3-Row

LEFT-HANDED

RIGHT-HANDED

1. Come up at **A**. Follow Step 1 of the cretan stitch 3-row (left) from *, with **B** and **C** angled back toward to **A**.

2. Follow Step 2 with **D** and **E** angled back toward **C** of the previous stitch.

3. Repeat from * to finish the row. To end the stitch, go down at **F**, either after Step 1 or Step 2.

Cretan Stitch Spacing Variation

Cretan stitch 4-row (page 114)

Cretan stitch 3-row (above left)

Use the same parallel horizontal row spacing but with a shorter distance between the vertical rows.

Cretan Stitch Short Tip

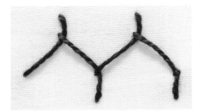

LEFT-HANDED

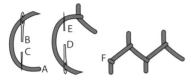

RIGHT-HANDED

Work this stitch between 3 or 4 horizontal rows.

1. Follow Step 1 of the cretan stitch (page 114, 115), making a short tip.

2. Follow Step 2 of the cretan stitch, making a short tip.

3. Repeat Steps 1 and 2 to finish the row. To end the stitch, go down at **F**.

Cretan Stitch with Loose Knot

LEFT-HANDED

RIGHT-HANDED

Work this stitch between 3 or 4 horizontal rows.

1. Follow Step 1 of the cretan stitch (page 114, 115). *Go under the base stitch only; wrap the working thread under the tip of the needle. Pull the thread firmly around the base stitch.

2. Follow Step 2 of the cretan stitch, repeat Step 1 above from *.

3. Repeat Steps 1 and 2 above to finish the row. To end the stitch, go down at **F**.

Cretan Stitch with Knot Tip

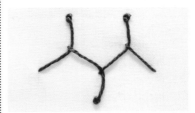

LEFT-HANDED

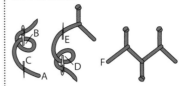

RIGHT-HANDED

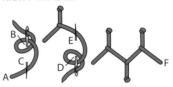

Work this stitch between 3 or 4 horizontal rows.

1. Come up at **A**. *Loop the thread over your finger and place the loop next to the fabric. Backstitch the needle in one motion down at an angle at **B** through the loop and up at **C**. Pull the thread tightly; then pull the needle through the fabric.

2. In one motion, go down at **D** and up at **E**, repeat Step 1 above from *.

3. Repeat Steps 1 and 2 above to finish the row. To end the stitch, go down at **F**.

Cretan Stitch Looped

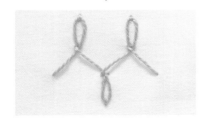

LEFT-HANDED

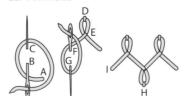

RIGHT-HANDED

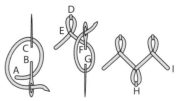

Work this stitch between 3 or 4 horizontal rows.

1. Come up at **A**. In one motion, go down at **B** and up at **C**. *Wrap the working thread under the eye and the tip of the needle and back to the base of the stitch. Pull the needle through the fabric. Go down at **D**.

2. Go down at **F** and up at **G**. Follow Step 1 from *, going down at **H**.

3. Repeat Steps 1 and 2 above to finish the row. To end the stitch, go down at **I**.

Cretan Stitch Double-Single

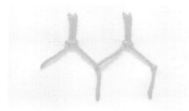

A

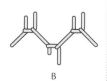

B

A. Follow Step 1 of the cretan stitch double tip (page 119). Follow Step 2 of the cretan stitch (page 114).

B. Follow Steps 1 and 2 of the cretan stitch double tip (page 119), working the second tip longer than the first tip. *Option:* Substitute the cretan stitch up and down (page 118) for the cretan stitch double.

Cretan Stitch Straight/Angled

Cretan stitch
4-row

Cretan stitch 3-row
spaced closer together

Work 1 cretan stitch (page 114, 115). Work 1 cretan stitch angled (page 115).

Cretan Stitch Angled Tips

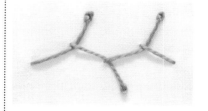

A. Cretan stitch with knot tip (page 116)

B. Cretan stitch looped (page 116)

Work this stitch between 3 or 4 horizontal rows.

Follow the directions for the above stitches using the needle positioning for the cretan stitch angled (page 115).

Cretan Stitch Capped

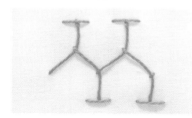

Work this stitch between 3 or 4 horizontal rows.

1. Stitch a row of cretan stitches (page 114, 115).

2. With the same or a different color of thread, work 1 straight stitch (page 43) from **E** to **F** across each stitch.

Left-handed version: *In Step 2, reverse* **E** *and* **F** *and vice versa.*

Steeple and Cross Stitch Row

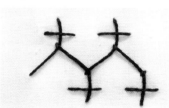

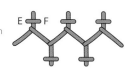

Work this stitch between 3 or 4 horizontal rows.

1. Stitch 1 row of cretan stitches (page 114, 115).

2. With the same or a different color of thread, work 1 straight stitch (page 43) from **E** to **F** across each stitch.

Left-handed version: *In Step 2, reverse* **E** *and* **F** *and vice versa.*

Cretan Stitch with Arrow Tip Detail

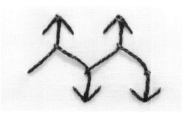

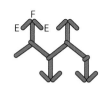

Work this stitch between 3 or 4 horizontal rows.

1. Stitch 1 row of cretan stitches (page 114, 115).

2. With the same or a different color of thread, work 2 straight stitches (page 43) from **E** to **F** across each stitch.

Left-handed version: *In Step 2, reverse* **E** *and* **F** *and vice versa.*

Cretan Stitch Laced

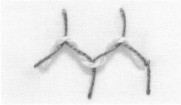

1. Stitch 1 row of cretan stitches (page 114).

2. With a different color of thread, come up next to the stitch at the beginning of the row. Thread the needle under and over the stitches, not through the fabric.

3. To end the stitch, go down next to the last stitch in the row.

Cretan Stitch Up and Down

1. Follow Step 1 of the cretan stitch (page 114). *In one motion, go down at **F** and up at **G**. Loop the working thread over the tip of the needle. Pull the needle through the fabric. Pass the needle under the loop and gently pull the thread to tighten.

2. Follow Step 2 of the cretan stitch, repeat Step 1 above from *.

3. Repeat Steps 1 and 2 above to finish the row. To end the stitch, go down **H**.

LEFT-HANDED

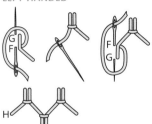

RIGHT-HANDED

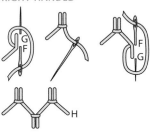

Cretan Stitch Offset Angle

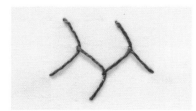

LEFT-HANDED

RIGHT-HANDED

Work this stitch between 3 or 4 horizontal rows.

1. Follow Step 1 of the cretan stitch (page 114, 115) with **B** (above **A** and angled away) and up at **C**.

2. Follow Step 2 of the cretan stitch with **D** (below **C** and angled away) and up at **E**.

3. Repeat Steps 1 and 2 above to finish the row. To end the stitch, go down at **F**.

Cretan Stitch with Feather Stitch

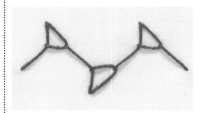

Work this stitch between 3 or 4 horizontal rows.

1. Follow Step 1 of the cretan stitch (page 114, 115). *In one motion, go down at **F** and up at **G**. Wrap the working thread under the tip of the needle. Pull the needle through the fabric.

2. Follow Step 2 of the cretan stitch and Step 1 above from *.

3. Repeat Steps 1 and 2 above to finish the row. To end the stitch, go down at **H**.

LEFT-HANDED

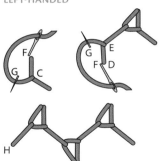

RIGHT-HANDED

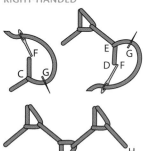

Cretan Stitch with Chain Stitch

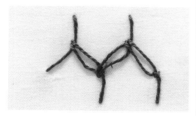

LEFT-HANDED

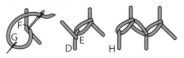

RIGHT-HANDED

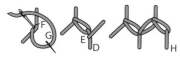

1. Follow Step 1 of the cretan stitch (page 114). *In one motion, go down at **F** and up at **G**. Wrap the working thread under the tip of the needle. Pull the needle through the fabric.

2. Follow Step 2 of the cretan stitch and Step 1 above from *.

3. Repeat Steps 1 and 2 above to finish the row. To end the stitch, go down at **H**.

Cretan Stitch Tip Variations

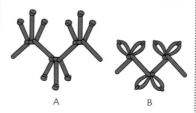

A. Follow the directions for the cretan stitch sprig tip (page 120), substituting the directions for the cretan stitch with knot tip (page 116) for the first and third tip.

B. Follow the directions for the cretan stitch forked tip (page 120), substituting the directions for the cretan stitch looped (page 116).

Cretan Stitch Double Tip

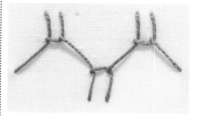

LEFT-HANDED   **RIGHT-HANDED**

Work this stitch between 3 or 4 horizontal rows.

1. Work 1 cretan stitch (page 114, 115). * In one motion, go down at **F** and up at **G**. Wrap the working thread under the tip of the needle. Pull the needle through the fabric.

2. Repeat Step 1 to finish the row, working the next set of stitches below or above and to the side of the first set of stitches. To end the stitch go down at **H**.

Cretan Stitch Triple Tip

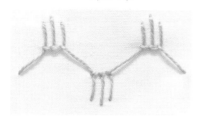

LEFT-HANDED   **RIGHT-HANDED**

1. Follow Step 1 of the cretan stitch double tip (above right). *Work the second tip slightly longer than the first. Work a third tip the same length as the first.

2. Repeat Step 1 to finish the row, working the next set of stitches below or above and to the side of the first set of stitches. To end the stitch, go down at **H**.

Cretan Stitch Forked Tip

LEFT-HANDED

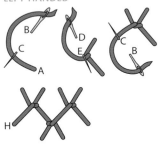

RIGHT-HANDED

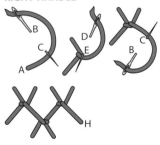

Work this stitch between 3 or 4 horizontal rows.

1. Come up at **A**. *In one motion, angle the stitch, going down at **B** and up at **C**. Pull the needle through the fabric. In one motion, angle the stitch, going down at **D** and up at **E**. Pull the needle through the fabric.

2. Repeat Step 1 from * to finish the row, working the next set of stitches below or above and to the side of the first set of stitches. To end the stitch go down at **H**.

Cretan Stitch Sprig Tip

LEFT-HANDED

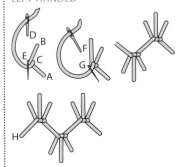

RIGHT-HANDED

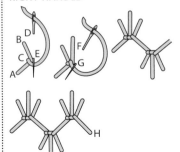

Work this stitch between 3 or 4 horizontal rows.

1. Come up at **A**. *In one motion, angle the stitch, going down at **B** and up at **C**. Pull the needle through the fabric. In one motion, go down at **D** and up at **E**, higher than the first stitch and straight. Pull the needle through the fabric. In one motion, angle the stitch, going down at **F** and up at **G**. Pull the needle through the fabric.

2. Repeat Step 1 from * to finish the row, working the next set of stitches below or above and to the side of the first set of stitches. To end the stitch, go down at **H**.

Cretan and Stem Stitches

LEFT-HANDED

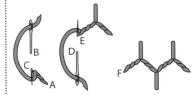

RIGHT-HANDED

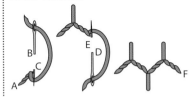

Work this stitch between 3 or 4 horizontal rows.

1. Come up at **A**. *Work 3 stem stitches (page 47). Work 1 cretan stitch (page 114, 115).

2. Repeat Step 1 from * to finish the row, working the next group of stitches to the side and below or above the previous stitch. To end the stitch, work 3 stem stitches and go down at **F**.

Variations: *Change the number of stem stitches or the type of cretan stitch.*

Cretan Stitch Looped and Chain Stitches

LEFT-HANDED

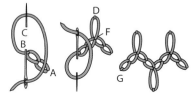

RIGHT-HANDED

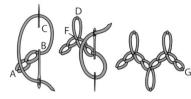

Work this stitch between 3 or 4 horizontal rows.

1. Work 2 chain stitches (page 67). Work 1 cretan stitch looped (page 116).

2. Repeat Step 1 to finish the row, working the next group of stitches to the side and below or above the previous stitch. To end the stitch, work 2 chain stitches and go down at **G**.

Variations: *Change the number of chain stitches or the type of cretan stitch.*

Cretan and Coral Stitches

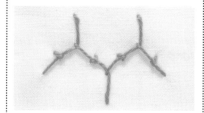

LEFT-HANDED

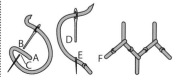

RIGHT-HANDED

Work this stitch between 3 or 4 horizontal rows.

1. Come up at **A**. *Hold the working thread straight. In one motion, go down at **B** and up at **C**. Wrap the working thread under the tip of the needle. Pull the needle through the fabric.

2. Work 1 cretan stitch (page 114, 115) from *, substituting points **D** and **E** for **B** and **C**.

3. Repeat Step 1 from * and Step 2 above to finish the row, working the next group of stitches to the side and below or above the previous stitch. To end the stitch, work 1 coral knot stitch and go down at **F**.

Note: *Reverse the coral knot stitch from the original version to use it for this stitch.*

Cretan and Blanket Stitches

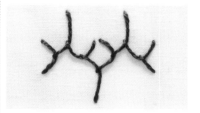

LEFT-HANDED   **RIGHT-HANDED**

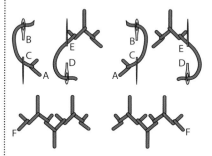

Work this stitch between 3 or 4 horizontal rows.

1. Work 1 blanket stitch (page 80). Follow Step 1 of the cretan stitch (page 114, 115) from *.

2. Work 1 blanket stitch. Follow Step 2 of the cretan stitch.

3. Repeat Steps 1 and 2 above to finish the row. To end the stitch, work 1 blanket stitch and go down at **F**.

Variations: *Change the number of blanket stitches or the type of cretan stitch.*

Cretan Stitch Overlaid

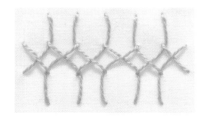

Row 1: Stitch 1 row of cretan stitch stitches (page 114). Turn the fabric.

Row 2: Stitch a second row, overlapping the stitches of the previous row.

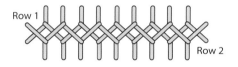

Variations: *Change the type of cretan stitch or use a different color of thread for row 2.*

CROSS STITCHES

General Information

These individual stitches can be used as a single stitch, combined to create a border row, or added to another stitch to create a larger component.

The following stitches are formed by coming up at point **A** and going down at point **B** to create a straight line. The stitch is completed by coming up at point **C** and going down at point **D**, crossing over the previous stitch. If the stitch has a detail, it would continue with point **E** and **F** stitches or more.

For a reference guide for a single stitch, use an erasable pen to draw 2 parallel lines or 4 points the length and width of the stitch.

For a reference guide and even spacing for a row of stitches, you could draw 2 lines the length and width of the row with an erasable pen and then mark off the lines in even intervals.

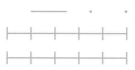

Cross Stitch

Elongated horizontally

Elongated vertically

1. Come up at **A** and go down at **B**.

2. Come up at **C** and go down at **D**, crossing over the first stitch.

Variations: *Change the length and/or height of the stitches.*

Cross Stitch Row

1. Come up at **A** and go down at **B**. Repeat this step across the row.

2. Come up at **C** and go down at **D**. Repeat this step across the row.

Variations: *Change the length and/or height of the stitches, or substitute a different color of thread in Step 2.*

Cross Stitch Variations

1. Stitch 1 cross stitch (page 122) following the illustrations below.

2. Follow any additional instructions.

Variations: *Change the length and/or height of the stitches.*

Cross stitch short cross

Cross stitch long arm

Repeat Step 2 of the cross stitch.

Cross stitch single-double

Cross stitch vertical

Cross stitch vertical offset

Stitch 1 straight stitch (page 43) from E to F, crossing over the middle of the first stitch.

Cross stitch with straight stitches

Cross and French knot stitches

Stitch 2-wrap French knots (page 54) in the same or a different color of thread.

Stitch 1 straight stitch (page 43) from E to F over each tip of the stitch.

Cross stitch capped

Stitch 2 straight stitches (page 43) from E to F above the crossed portion of the stitch.

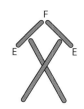

Cross stitch with arrow tip detail

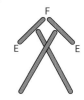

Cross stitch short cross with arrow tip detail

Crossed Pistil Stitch

 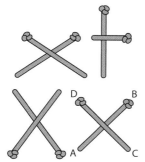

Stitch 1 pistil stitch (page 44) from **A** to **B**. Stitch a second stitch, crossing over the first from **C** to **D**.

Optional: *Stitch a short straight stitch over the crossed portion of the stitch.*

Variations: *Change the length or position of the crossed portion of the stitch.*

Crossed Lazy Daisy Stitch Long Arm

Stitch 1 lazy daisy stitch with long arm (page 60) from **A** to **B**. Stitch a second stitch, crossing over the first from **C** to **D**.

Optional: *Stitch a short straight stitch over the crossed portion of the stitch.*

Variations: *Change the length or position of the crossed portion of the stitch.*

Crossed Fly Stitch Long Tail

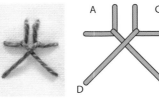

Stitch 1 fly stitch with long tail (page 92) from **A** to **B**. Stitch a second stitch, crossing over the first from **C** to **D**.

Optional: *Stitch a short straight stitch over the crossed portion of the stitch.*

Variations: *Change the length or position of the crossed portion of the stitch.*

Woven Cross Stitch

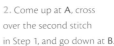

1. Stitch 2 straight stitches (page 43): the first stitch from **A** to **B** and the second stitch from **C** to **D**.

2. Come up at **A**, cross over the second stitch in Step 1, and go down at **B**.

3. Come up at **C**. Pass the needle over the stitch in Step 2 and under the first stitch in Step 1; go down at **D**.

Crosshatch Stitch

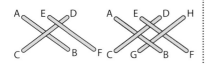

1. Work 1 cross stitch (page 122) elongated horizontally. Come up at **E** (between **D** and **A**) and go down at **F**.

2. Come up at **G** (below **E**). Thread the needle under the stitch and then over the previous stitch; go down at **H**.

Magic Cross Stitch

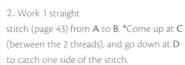

1. Thread the needle with 2 colors of the same thread. Knot the tails together.

2. Work 1 straight stitch (page 43) from **A** to **B**. *Come up at **C** (between the 2 threads), and go down at **D** to catch one side of the stitch.

3. Repeat from * to catch the opposite side of the stitch.

Cross Stitch Twisted

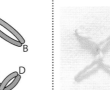

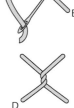

1. Come up at **A** and go down at **B**.

2. Come up at **C**. Thread the needle under and then over the previous stitch; go down at **D**, working from right to left.

Left-handed version: *Reverse the direction of the stitches.*

Crossed Lazy Daisy Stitch

 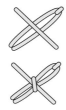

1. Stitch 1 lazy daisy stitch (page 60).

2. Stitch 1 straight stitch (page 43) the same length and width, crossed over the first stitch.

3. Stitch 1 short straight stitch from across the middle of the crossed section.

Crossed Star Stitch

1. Stitch 1 cross stitch (page 122).

2. Stitch 1 cross stitch vertical (page 123) over the first stitch using a different color of thread.

Variation: *Change the length of the stitches.*

Cross and Straight Stitch Shapes

1. Stitch 1 cross stitch (page 122).

2. Stitch straight stitches (page 43) to connect the tips and the center of the cross stitch using a different color of thread.

Hourglass

Diamond

Bow

Cross Stitch Vertical with Cross Stitch Details

1. Stitch 1 cross stitch vertical (page 123).

2. Stitch cross stitch (page 122) details into each open portion of the stitch using a different color of thread.

Variations: *Change the length or type of cross stitch, or the position of the cross stitch details.*

Cross Stitch Vertical Shapes

Diamond

Square

Base for either shape:
Stitch 1 cross stitch vertical (page 123). Stitch a straight stitch (page 43) or cross stitch (page 122) over the crossed section.

• **Diamond:** Stitch 4 lazy daisy stitches (page 60) to connect the tips of the cross stitch using a different color of thread.

• **Square:** Stitch 4 fly stitches (page 92) to connect the tips of the cross stitch using a different color of thread.

Cross Stitch Doubled

1. Stitch 1 cross stitch (page 122).

2. Stitch 1 cross stitch vertical (page 123) and smaller over the first stitch using a different color of thread.

Cross Stitch Doubled and Fly Stitch Shapes

Base for either stitch: Stitch 1 crossed star stitch (page 125). Stitch 1 cross stitch (page 122) into the center.

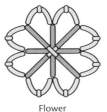

Flower

- **Flower:** Stitch 8 fly stitches (page 92) to connect the tips of the cross stitches using a different color of thread.

Butterfly

- **Butterfly:** Stitch 4 fly stitches (page 92) to connect the tips of the cross stitches using a different color of thread.

Four-Corner Cross Stitch

A   C

E   G

D   B

H   F

1. Draw in the template.

2. Work straight stitches (page 43) from **A** to **B**, **C** to **D**, **E** to **F**, and **G** to **H**.

Four-Corner Cross Stitch with Details

French knot stitch

Fly stitch

Lazy daisy stitch

1. Follow the directions for the four-corner cross stitch (above middle).

2. With a different color of thread, stitch 2-wrap French knot stitches (page 54), fly stitches (page 92), or lazy daisy stitches (page 60).

Four-Corner Cross Stitch Star

Base: Stitch 1 four-corner cross stitch (left). Stitch 4 straight stitches (page 43) over the crossed portion of the stitch using a different color of thread.

Points: Stitch 4 fly stitches (page 92) to connect the tips of the cross stitches using a different color of thread.

Cross and Fly Stitch Stars

Base: Stitch 1 cross stitch (page 122).

Points: Stitch 4 fly stitches (page 92) the same size or different sizes to connect the tips of the cross stitches using a different color of thread.

Crossed Wing Stitch

LEFT-HANDED   RIGHT-HANDED

1. Come up at A and go down at **B**.

2. Come up at **C**. Cross over the previous stitch and then under the stitch and up. Cross over this new stitch; then go down at **D**.

3. To finish the row, repeat Steps 1 and 2, with **A** crossing over the stitch in Step 2.

Thorn Stitch

LEFT-HANDED

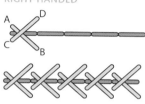

RIGHT-HANDED

1. Stitch a row of backstitches (page 48) or long straight stitches (page 43).

2. Come up at **A** and go down at **B**. Come up at **C** and go down at **D**.

3. Repeat Step 2 to finish the row.

Cross Stitch Row Netted

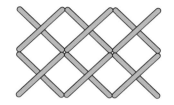

1. Stitch 1 row of cross stitches (page 122).

2. Stitch a second row, with the spokes mirroring the first.

Variations: *Change the length or type of the stitch, or work the stitch within the open section of each cross.*

Change the type of cross stitch or use a different color of thread for row 2.

Cross Stitch Row Overlaid

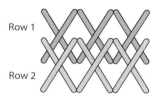

Row 1
Row 2

Row 1: Stitch 1 row of cross stitches (page 122).

Row 2: Stitch a second row, overlapping the stitches of the previous row.

Variations: *Change the type of cross stitch or use a different color of thread for row 2.*

Cross Stitch Rows with Variations

1. Stitch 1 row of cross stitches (page 122).

2. Stitch a second row of stitches in a different color following the suggestions below.

Cross stitch row with stem stitches

Stitch the stem stitch (page 47) over each crossed portion of the stitch.

Chained cross stitch row

Stitch a row of chain stitches (page 67) through the crossed portion of the stitch.

Cross stitch row capped

1. Stitch 1 straight stitch (page 43) over the crossed portion of the stitch.

2. Stitch 1 straight stitch across the tips of a stitch, alternating between the top or bottom portion of the stitch.

Cross and fly stitch row

1. Stitch 1 fly stitch (page 92) into the tips of a stitch, alternating between the top and bottom portion of the stitch.

HERRINGBONE STITCHES

General Information

These continuous stitches can be used for a border row or to create a shape. After the stitch is formed, individual stitches can be added to the tips or around the base to create a larger design.

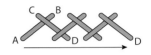

The basic stitch is formed by coming up at point **A** and then, in one motion, going down at point **B** and coming up at point **C**, forming a straight stitch. The stitch continues with point **D**, then back to point **A**. The stitch is worked continuously and would end at point **B** or **D** unless otherwise noted. This stitch can also be worked in individual stab motions.

HERRINGBONE STITCH SPACING GUIDES

For a reference guide and even spacing, you could draw 2 parallel lines the length and width of the row with an erasable pen and then mark off the lines at even intervals.

The basic herringbone stitches can be made easier if you first practice with this grid method. Draw 2 horizontal parallel lines the length and width of the row with an erasable pen. Mark the spacing vertically by half the measurement of the width of the row. Number the horizontal lines as shown, number the vertical lines 1–3, and repeat. Refer to the basic herringbone stitch instructions listed below.

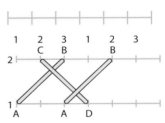

Note: *The mark and line numbers will change depending on the stitch. As a general reference, skip 1 mark and then backstitch B and C on the line below or above A; A of the new stitch is below the same mark as B of the previous stitch.*

Left-handed version: *The numbering on the horizontal lines should be listed beginning on the right-hand side. The points on the example of the stitch would then be reversed.*

Herringbone Stitch

Work this stitch between 2 horizontal rows.

1. Come up at **A**. *Backstitch the needle in one motion down at **B** and up at **C**. Pull the needle through the fabric. Repeat from *, going down at **D** and up at **A**.

2. Repeat Step 1 to finish the row. To end the stitch, go down at **B** or **D**.

LEFT-HANDED   **RIGHT-HANDED**

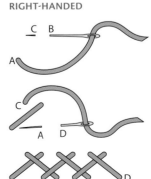

Herringbone Stitch Short-Long

LEFT-HANDED

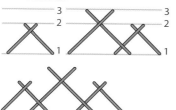

RIGHT-HANDED

Work this stitch between 3 horizontal rows.

1. Follow the directions for the herringbone stitch (page 128). Work the stitches in the pattern below:

- **Short stitch:** Work the stitch between the first and second lines.

- **Long stitch:** Work the stitch between the first and third lines.

2. Repeat Step 1 to finish the row.

Herringbone Long Arm Stitch

LEFT-HANDED

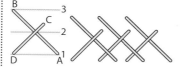

RIGHT-HANDED

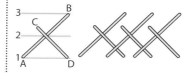

Work this stitch between 3 horizontal rows.

1. Come up at **A** and go down at **B**. Come up at **C** and go down at **D**.

2. Repeat Step 1 to finish the row.

Herringbone Stitch Boxed

LEFT-HANDED

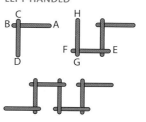

RIGHT-HANDED

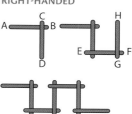

1. Come up at **A** and go down at **B**. Come up at **C** and go down at **D**.

2. Come up at **E** and go down at **F**. Come up at **G** and go down at **H**.

3. Repeat Steps 1 and 2 to finish the row. The stitch can end with **B**, **D**, **F**, or **H**.

Herringbone Stitch Elongated

Work this stitch between 2 horizontal rows.

1. Come up at **A** and go down at **B** using the line markings.

2. Come up at **C** and go down at **D** using the dot markings.

3. Repeat Steps 1 and 2 to finish the row.

LEFT-HANDED

RIGHT-HANDED

Herringbone Stitch Condensed

LEFT-HANDED

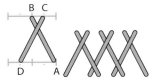

RIGHT-HANDED

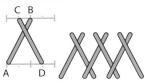

Work this stitch between 2 horizontal rows.

1. Come up at **A** and go down at **B** using the line markings.

2. Come up at **C** and go down at **D** using the dot markings.

3. Repeat Steps 1 and 2 to finish the row.

Herringbone Double Stitch

LEFT-HANDED

RIGHT-HANDED

Work this stitch between 2 horizontal rows.

1. Come up at **A** and go down at **B**. Work a second stitch next to the first.

2. Come up at **C** and go down at **D**. Work a second stitch next to the first.

3. Repeat Steps 1 and 2 to finish the row.

Herringbone Stitch Cascade

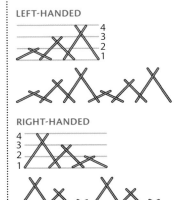

Work this stitch between 4 horizontal rows.

1. Follow the directions for the herringbone stitch (page 128). Work the stitches in the pattern below:

- **Long stitch:** Work the stitch between the first and fourth lines.

- **Medium stitch:** Work the stitch between the first and third lines.

- **Short stitch:** Work the stitch between the first and second lines.

2. Repeat Step 1 to finish the row.

Herringbone Stitch Netted

1. Stitch 1 row of herringbone stitches (page 128). Turn the fabric.

2. Stitch a second row, with the cross sections mirroring the first.

Variations: *Change the length or type of the stitch or the color of the thread in the second row.*

Herringbone Stitch Twisted

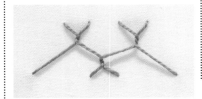

Work this stitch between 2 horizontal rows.

1. Come up at **A** and go down at **B**.

2. Come up at **C**. Thread the needle under and then over the previous stitch; go down at **D**.

3. Repeat Steps 1 and 2 to finish the row. To end the stitch, go down at **D**.

LEFT-HANDED

RIGHT-HANDED

Herringbone Stitch with Loose Knot

LEFT-HANDED

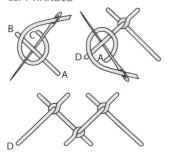

RIGHT-HANDED

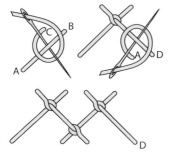

Work this stitch between 2 horizontal rows.

1. Come up at **A** and go down at **B**.

2. Come up at **C**. Go under the previous stitch and wrap the working thread under the tip of the needle. Pull the thread firmly around the base stitch. Go down at **D**.

3. Repeat Steps 1 and 2 to finish the row. To end the stitch, go down at **D**.

Herringbone–Lazy Daisy Long Arm Stitch

LEFT-HANDED

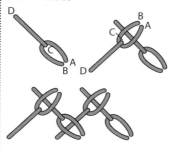

RIGHT-HANDED

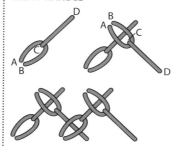

1. Stitch 1 lazy daisy long arm stitch (page 60) at an angle.

2. Stitch a second stitch, crossing over the previous stitch.

3. Repeat Step 2 to finish the row.

Herringbone and Pistil Stitch

LEFT-HANDED

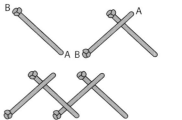

RIGHT-HANDED

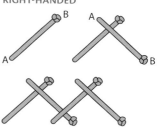

1. Stitch 1 pistil stitch (page 44) at an angle from **A** to **B**.

2. Stitch a second stitch, crossing over the previous stitch, from **A** to **B**.

3. Repeat Step 2 to finish the row.

Herringbone and Coral Stitches

LEFT-HANDED

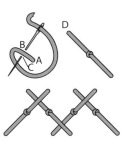

RIGHT-HANDED

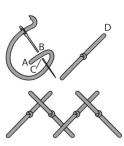

1. Come up at **A**. Hold the working thread straight. In one motion, go down at **B** and come up at **C**. Wrap the working thread under the tip of the needle. Pull the needle through the fabric. Go down at **D**.

2. Repeat Step 1, crossing over the previous stitch to finish the row.

Note: *Reverse the coral knot stitch from the original version to use it for this stitch.*

Herringbone and Blanket Stitches

LEFT-HANDED

RIGHT-HANDED

1. Come up at **A**. Follow Step 1 of the blanket stitch (page 80) from *, working the stitch at an angle. Go down at **D**.

2. Repeat Step 1, crossing over the previous stitch to finish the row.

Herringbone Stitch Overlaid

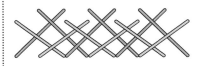

Row 1: Stitch 1 row of herringbone stitches (page 128).

Row 2: Stitch a second row that's shorter than the first, overlapping the stitches of the previous row.

Variations: *Change the type of herringbone stitch or use a second color of thread for row 2.*

Herringbone Stitch Laced

1. Stitch 1 row of herringbone stitches (page 128).

2. With a different color of thread, come up next to the stitch at the beginning of the row. Thread the needle over and under the stitches, not through the fabric.

3. To end the row, go down next to the last stitch in the row.

Herringbone Stitch with Details

1. Stitch 1 row of herringbone stitches (page 128).

2. With a different color of thread, stitch straight stitches (page 43) in any of the patterns shown.

Herringbone Stitch Capped

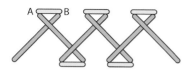

1. Stitch 1 row of herringbone stitches (page 128).

2. With the same or a different color of thread, stitch 1 straight stitch (page 43) from **A** to **B** over each open crossed section.

Left-handed version: *In Step 2, reverse* **A** *for* **B** *and vice versa.*

Herringbone Stitch with Arrow Tip Detail

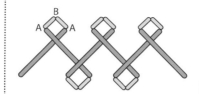

1. Stitch 1 row of herringbone stitches (page 128).

2. With the same or a different color of thread, stitch 2 straight stitches (page 43) from **A** to **B** over each open crossed section.

Herringbone and Cross Stitch Single

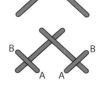

1. Stitch 1 set of herringbone stitches (page 128).

2. With the same or a different color of thread, work 2 straight stitches (page 43) from **A** to **B** across the bottom portion of the stitch.

Herringbone and Cross Stitch Single Variations

A   B   C

A. Stitch 1 set of herringbone double stitches (page 130). Follow Step 2 of the herringbone and cross stitch single (above right), with 2 stitches per cross.

B. Stitch 1 herringbone and cross stitch single; add straight stitch (page 43) details.

C. Follow Step 1 of the herringbone and cross stitch single. Add a pistil stitch (page 44) for Step 2. Add additional pistil stitch details.

Note: *Work with the same color or a different color of thread for the detail stitches.*

Herringbone Random Filling Stitch

Work a row of herringbone stitches (page 128), randomly varying the heights, spacing, and angles.

Herringbone Stitch with Variations

Stitch 1 row of herringbone stitches (page 128).

Stitch a second row of stitches in a different color following the suggestions below. Choose a different herringbone stitch or use a variation of the second stitch.

Herringbone and French knot stitches

Stitch 3-wrap French knot stitches (page 54) between the tips and under the crossed portion of the stitch.

Herringbone with pistil stitch details

Stitch pistil stitches (page 44) along the bottom tips of the stitch.

Herringbone stitch with lazy daisy stitch details

Stitch lazy daisy stitches (page 60) across the crossed section of the stitch or from the tips of the stitch.

Herringbone and chain stitches

Stitch a row of chain stitches (page 67) mirroring the diagonal line.

Herringbone stitch with blanket stitch overlay

Stitch a row of blanket stitches (page 80) across the bottom row.

Herringbone and fly stitches

Stitch fly stitches (page 92) around each crossed section.

Herringbone stitch and fly stitch long tail

Stitch fly stitches with long tails (page 92) at an angle across the row.

Herringbone and cross stitches

Stitch cross stitch long arm (page 123) across the row.

CAPPED STITCHES

General Information

These individual stitches can be used as a single stitch, combined to create a border row, or added to another stitch to create a larger component.

Each of these unique stitches are formed with one or more individual stitches. The stitches can be worked in separate stab motions by coming up at point **A** and going down at point **B** to create a straight line. If the stitch has a detail, it would continue with point **C** and **D** stitches or more.

Or the stitches can be worked by coming up at point **A** and then, in one motion, going down at point **B** and coming up at point **C**, which catches the loop formed by points **A** and **B**. The stitch would end with a point **D**. If the stitch has a detail, it would continue with point **E** and **F** stitches or more.

For a reference guide, use an erasable pen to draw 2 lines or 3 points the width and length of the stitch.

Capped Bar Stitch

LEFT-HANDED

RIGHT-HANDED

1. Come up at **A**. In one motion, go down at **B** and come up at **C** (**C** is between **A** and **B** under the line formed). Pull the needle through the fabric with the thread below the stitch.

2. To end the stitch, go down at **D**.

Capped Bar with Loose Knot Stitch

LEFT-HANDED

RIGHT-HANDED

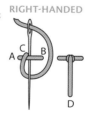

1. Follow Step 1 of the capped bar stitch (left); as you pull the needle through the fabric, bring the thread above the stitch.

2. Go under the first stitch, and wrap the working thread under the tip of the needle. Pull the thread firmly around the stitch.

3. To end the stitch, go down at **D**.

Capped Lazy Daisy Stitch

LEFT-HANDED

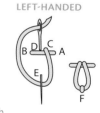

RIGHT-HANDED

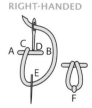

1. Follow Step 1 of the capped bar stitch (left); as you pull the needle through the fabric, bring the thread above the stitch.

2. In one motion, go down at **D** and up at **E**. Wrap the working thread under the tip of the needle. Pull the needle through the fabric.

3. To end the stitch, go down at **F**.

Capped Fly Stitch

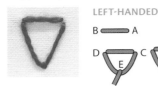

LEFT-HANDED

RIGHT-HANDED

1. Come up at **A** and go down at **B**.

2. Come up at **C**; in one motion, go down at **D** and come up at **E**. Wrap the working thread under the tip of the needle. Pull the needle through the fabric.

3. To end the stitch, go down at **F**.

Capped Pistil Stitch

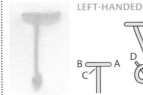

LEFT-HANDED

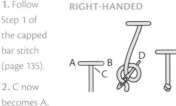

RIGHT-HANDED

1. Follow Step 1 of the capped bar stitch (page 135).

2. C now becomes A. Follow the directions for the Chinese knot stitch (page 55), going down at **D**.

Bar-Fly Stitch

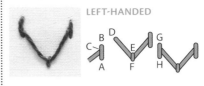

LEFT-HANDED

RIGHT-HANDED

1. Come up at **A**. In one motion, go down at **B** and come up at **C** (**C** is under **A** and **B** under the line formed). Pull the needle through the fabric with the thread to the side.

2. In one motion, go down at **D** and come up at **E**. Wrap the working thread under the tip of the needle. Pull the needle through the fabric. Go down at **F**.

3. To finish the stitch, come up at **G** and go down at **H**.

Capped Stitch Flowers

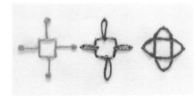

Capped pistil stitch (above middle)

Capped lazy daisy stitch (page 135)

Capped fly stitch (above left)

Choose one of the flowers. Draw a square. Follow the directions for the stitch listed, working the petals consecutively.

Capped Bar Stitch Row

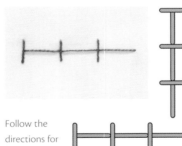

Follow the directions for the capped bar stitch (page 135), working the stitches along a drawn or imaginary line.

Variations: *Change the length, width, or angle of the stitch.*

Capped Bar with Loose Knot Stitch Row

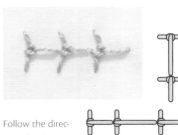

Follow the directions for the capped bar with loose knot stitch (page 135), working the stitches along a drawn or imaginary line.

Variations: *Change the length, width, or angle of the stitch.*

Capped Pistil Stitch Row

Follow the directions for the capped pistil stitch (page 136), working the stitches along a drawn or imaginary line.

Variations: *Change the length, width, or angle of the stitch.*

Capped Lazy Daisy Stitch Row

Follow the directions for the capped lazy daisy stitch (page 135), working the stitches along a drawn or imaginary line.

Variations: *Change the length, width, or angle of the stitch, or the type of lazy daisy stitch.*

Capped Fly Stitch Row

Follow the directions for the capped fly stitch (page 136), working the stitches along a drawn or imaginary line.

Vertical or horizontal row with fly stitch

Variations: *Change the length, width, or angle of the stitch, or the type of fly stitch.*

Vertical or horizontal row with fly stitch straight edge (page 93)

Capped Fly Stitch Star

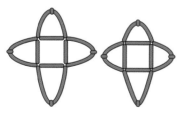

Draw a square. Follow the directions for the capped fly stitch (page 136). Work the points consecutively in all the same length or varied lengths.

Barbell Stitch

1. Follow Steps 1 and 2 of the capped bar stitch (page 135).

2. Come up at E and go down at F.

Left-handed version: *In Step 2, reverse E and F and vice versa.*

Barbell Stitch Row

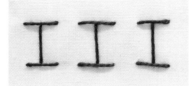

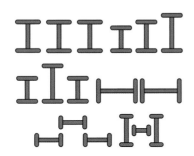

Follow the directions for the barbell stitch (page 137), working the stitches along a drawn or imaginary line.

Variations: *Change the length, width, or angle of the stitch.*

Barbell Stitch Angled

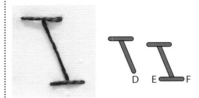

1. Follow Step 1 of the barbell stitch (page 137), angling the stitch to **D**.

2. Follow Step 2 of the barbell stitch.

Left-handed version: *In Step 2, reverse* **E** *and* **F** *and vice versa.*

Barbell Stitch Angled Row

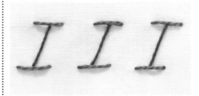

Single

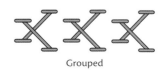

Grouped

Follow the directions for the barbell stitch angled (left), working the stitches along a drawn or imaginary line.

Variations: *Change the length, width, or angle of the stitch, or combine a group of stitches.*

Barbell Stitch Angled Crossed Row

Individual stitches: Work 1 barbell stitch angled (above middle) along a drawn or imaginary line. Work a second stitch across the first.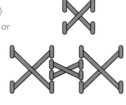

Connected row: Work 1 individual stitch. Work each consecutive stitch sharing the bar from the previous stitch.

Variations: *Change the length or width of the stitch.*

Barbell Stitch Zigzag Row

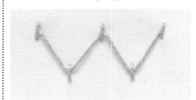

Follow the directions for the barbell stitch angled (above middle), working the stitches along a drawn or imaginary line.

Note: *You can use Vine B (page 51) for accurate spacing.*

Variations: *Change the length, width, or angle of the stitch, or have the following stitch share a cap from the previous stitch.*

CHEVRON STITCHES

General Information

These continuous stitches can be used for a border row or to create a shape. After the stitch is formed, individual stitches can be added to the tips or around the base to create a larger design.

The basic stitch is formed by coming up at point **A**. The needle is backstitched in one motion down at **B** and up at **C**; this creates a bar across the bottom of the stitch. The needle is backstitched down at **D** and up at **E**, then backstitched down at **F** and up at **D**; this creates a bar at the top of the stitch. This stitch can also be worked in individual stab motions.

CHEVRON STITCH SPACING GUIDES

For a reference guide and even spacing, use an erasable pen to draw 2 parallel lines the length and width of the row, and then mark off the lines at even intervals.

The basic chevron stitches can be made easier if you first practice with this grid method. With an erasable pen, draw 2 horizontal parallel lines the length and width of the row. Mark the spacing vertically the same measurement of the width of the row. Place a dot in between the vertical spaces.

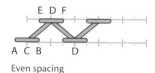

Even spacing

With an erasable pen, draw 2 horizontal parallel lines the length and width of the row. Mark the spacing vertically by half the measurement of the width of the row. Place a dot in between the vertical spaces.

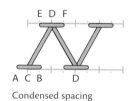

Condensed spacing

With an erasable pen, draw 2 horizontal parallel lines the length and width of the row. Mark the spacing vertically by half the measurement of the width of the row. Place a dot in between every third vertical space.

Left-handed version: *The numbering on the horizontal lines should be listed beginning on the right-hand side. The points on the example of the stitch would then be reversed.*

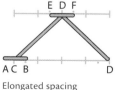

Elongated spacing

Chevron Stitch

LEFT-HANDED

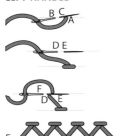

RIGHT-HANDED

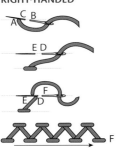

Work this stitch between 2 horizontal lines.

1. Come up at **A**. Backstitch in one motion down at **B** and up at **C**. Pull the needle through the fabric.

2. Backstitch in one motion down at **D** and up at **E**. Pull the needle through the fabric. Backstitch in one motion down at **F** and up at **D**.

3. Repeat Step 2 to finish the row, alternating the stitches between the lines. To end the stitch, go down at **F**.

Rolling Hills Stitch

LEFT-HANDED

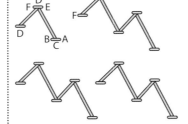

RIGHT-HANDED

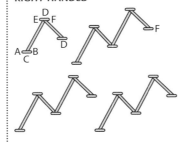

Work this stitch between 4 horizontal lines.

1. Follow Steps 1 and 2 of the chevron stitch (left), working the stitch lengths in this pattern: long, short, long, short. To end the stitch, go down at **F**.

2. Repeat Step 1 above to finish the row.

Chevron Stitch Short-Long

LEFT-HANDED

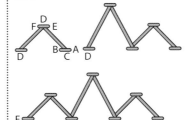

RIGHT-HANDED

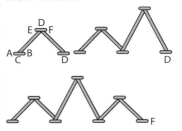

Work this stitch between 3 horizontal lines.

1. Follow Steps 1 and 2 of the chevron stitch (left), working the stitch lengths in this pattern: 2 short, 2 long.

2. Repeat Step 1 above to finish the row. To end the stitch, go down at **F**.

Mountain and Valley Stitch

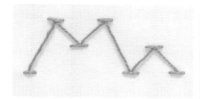

LEFT-HANDED

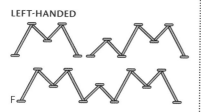

RIGHT-HANDED

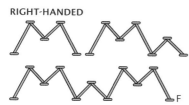

Work this stitch between 3 horizontal lines.

1. Follow Steps 1 and 2 of the chevron stitch (page 140), working the stitch lengths in this pattern:

• **First group:** Long, short, short, long

• **Second group:** Short, short

2. Repeat Step 1 above to finish the row. To end the stitch, go down at **F**.

Chevron Stitch Bar Length Variations

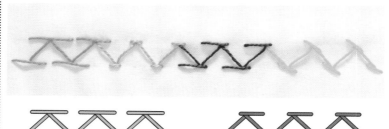

A. Elongated bar

C. Offset bar

B. Shortened bar

D. Angled bar

Follow the directions for the chevron stitch (page 140) with the bar in different lengths, positions, or angles.

Chevron Stitch Condensed

Follow the directions for the chevron stitch (page 140), working the stitches closer together.

Chevron Stitch Elongated

Follow the directions for the chevron stitch (page 140), working the stitches farther apart.

Chevron Stitch Overlaid

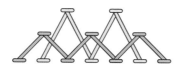

1. Stitch 1 row of chevron stitches (page 140).

2. Stitch a second row that's shorter than the first, overlapping the stitches of the previous row.

Variations: *Change the type of cretan stitch or use a different color of thread for the second row.*

Chevron Stitch Netted

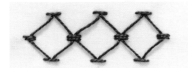

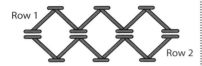

Row 1

Row 2

1. Stitch 1 row of chevron stitches (page 140). Turn the fabric.

2. Stitch a second row, with the stitches mirroring the first.

Variations: Change the type of chevron stitch, use a different color of thread for row 2, or share a bar from the previous row.

Chevron Stitch with Loose Knot

1. Follow Step 1 of the chevron stitch (page 140), *with the thread coming out below the bar. Go under the stitch, and wrap the working thread under the tip of the needle. Pull the thread firmly around the base stitch.

2. Follow Step 2 of the chevron stitch. Follow Step 1 above from *.

3. Repeat Step 2 above altering the stitches between the lines to finish the row. To end the stitch, go down at **G**.

LEFT-HANDED

RIGHT-HANDED

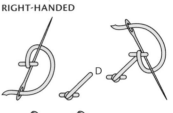

Chevron and Pistil Stitch

1. Follow Step 1 of the chevron stitch (page 140). C now becomes A. Follow the directions for the Chinese knot stitch (page 55), going down at **D**.

2. Come up at **E**. Backstitch in one motion down at **F** and up at **G**.

3. Repeat Steps 1 and 2 to finish the row. To end the stitch, go down at **F**.

LEFT-HANDED

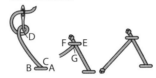

RIGHT-HANDED

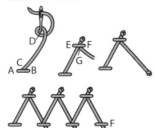

Sawtooth Stitch

LEFT-HANDED

RIGHT-HANDED

1. Follow Steps 1 and 2 of the chevron stitch (page 140), working the stitch positions in this pattern: angled, straight.

2. Repeat Step 1 above to finish the row.

Sawtooth Stitch Variation

LEFT-HANDED

RIGHT-HANDED

Work this stitch between 3 horizontal lines.

1. Follow Steps 1 and 2 of the chevron stitch (page 140), working the stitch length and position in this order:

- **First group:** Angled short, straight long
- **Second group:** Angled short, straight short

2. Go down at **F**.

3. Repeat Steps 1 and 2 above to finish the row.

Sawtooth Stitch Plaited

LEFT-HANDED

RIGHT-HANDED

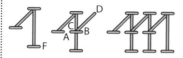

Work this stitch between 3 horizontal lines.

1. Follow Steps 1 and 2 of the chevron stitch (page 140), working the stitch length and position in this order: angled short, straight long. Go down at **F**.

2. Repeat Step 1 above to finish the row, working the beginning of the next stitch over the previous straight long stitch.

Chevron Stitch M-W

LEFT-HANDED

RIGHT-HANDED

Work this stitch between 3 horizontal lines.

1. Follow Steps 1 and 2 of the chevron stitch (page 140), working the stitch length and position in this order:

- **First group:** Straight, angled short, angled short, straight
- **Second group:** Angled short, angled short

2. Repeat Step 1 above to finish the row.

Chevron Stitch Double Thread

LEFT-HANDED

RIGHT-HANDED

Work this stitch between 2 horizontal lines.

1. Thread the needle with 2 colors of the same thread. Knot the tails together.

2. Work 1 straight stitch (page 43) from **A** to **B**.

3. Come up at **C** (between the 2 threads) and go down at **D**.

4. Repeat Steps 2 and 3 to finish the row, alternating between lines. To end the stitch, go down at **B**.

Chevron and Lazy Daisy Long Arm Stitch

LEFT-HANDED

RIGHT-HANDED

1. Follow Step 1 of the chevron stitch (page 140). *Work 1 lazy daisy long arm stitch (page 60). Go down at **D**.

2. Follow Step 2 of the chevron stitch.

3. Repeat from * to finish the row, alternating the stitches between the lines. To end the stitch, go down at **F**.

Chevron and Stem Stitches

LEFT-HANDED

RIGHT-HANDED

1. Follow Step 1 of the chevron stitch (page 140). *Stitch a row of stem stitches at an angle (page 47); go down at **D**.

2. Come up at **E**. In one motion, go down at **F** and up at **D**.

3. Repeat from * to finish the row, alternating between lines. To end the stitch, go down at **F**.

Chevron and Fly Stitch Long Tail

LEFT-HANDED

RIGHT-HANDED

1. Follow Steps 1 and 2 of the chevron stitch (page 140).

2. Work 1 fly stitch long tail (page 92). Go down at **D**.

3. Repeat Steps 1 and 2 above to finish the row. To end the stitch, go down at **F**.

Chevron Stitch with Variations

1. Stitch 1 row of chevron stitches (page 140).

2. In a different color, add a second row in your choice of stitches.

Variations: *Choose a different chevron stitch or a variation of the second stitch.*

Chevron stitch with straight stitch (page 43) details

Chevron stitch with 3-wrap French knot (page 54) details

Chevron stitch with lazy daisy stitch (page 60) details

Chevron stitch with fly stitch (pages 92, 93) details

Chevron stitch with cross stitch (pages 122, 123) details

EMBELLISHMENT STITCHES

General Information

These individual stitches can be used as a single stitch, combined to create a border row, or added to another stitch to create a larger component. These stitches can be worked with seed beads and larger beads.

Single Bead Stitch

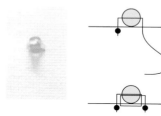

1. Come up and thread 1 bead onto the needle, placing the bead against the fabric. *Go down beyond the edge of the bead.

2. Come up and thread the needle through the bead a second time. Repeat Step 1 from *. Knot the thread after every 4 stitches.

Grouped Bead Stitch

Follow the directions for the single bead stitch (left), but with 2 or 3 beads of the same size. Knot the thread after every 2 stitches.

Bead Combination Stitch

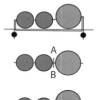

1. Follow the directions for the single bead stitch (left), but with a group of different sizes and shapes of beads.

2. Come up at **A** (between the large and small beads) and go down at **B** to couch the bead thread. Knot the thread after every 2 stitches.

Stacked Bead Stitch

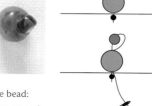

Base bead: Come up and thread 1 large bead onto the needle, placing the bead against the fabric.

Stopper bead: Thread a smaller bead onto the needle. Holding onto the bead, pass the needle back through the base bead and down. Knot the thread.

Beaded Charms

Front-to-back-hole charm stitch: Follow the directions for the stacked bead stitch (left); substitute the charm for the larger bead. Knot the thread.

Top-to-bottom-hole charm stitch: Follow the directions for the bead combination stitch (left) with the charm in the middle of the group; couch on either side of the charm. Knot the thread.

Stitched Buttons

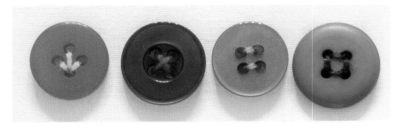

The holes of the button can be stitched in a variety of patterns using perle cotton or cotton floss.

Beaded Buttons

Stitch the holes of the button using seed beads, following the directions for the grouped bead stitch with 3 or more beads (page 145).

Stacked Buttons

Stitch a small button on top of a large button.

Clustered Buttons

Stitch buttons clustered into a group.

Button Spiders

Head and body: 1 button for each

Legs: Fly stitch offset (page 92)

Body: 1 button

Legs: Pistil stitch (page 44)

Button Bug

Body: 1 button

Wings: Lazy daisy stitches (page 60)

Antennae and legs: Pistil stitch (page 44)

Design Workshop

Embroidered Chorus

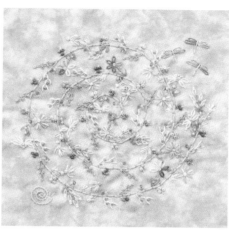

Embroidered Spiral

Embroidered Fan

Embroidered Heart

EMBROIDERED BASE DESIGNS

The construction of the fabric base will determine the overall design of the embroidery and embellishments. The fabric base can begin as a solid-color wholecloth base, a base with one or more printed fabrics, or a foundation strip- or crazy-pieced design. Additional elements of design such as ribbons, laces, trims, or appliqués and embellishments (like beads, buttons, or charms) can be added to offer more embroidery and embellishment opportunities.

WHOLECLOTH

The embroidery design for a solid piece of fabric can be worked in a large pattern, one with smaller vignettes, or entirely free-form throughout the base. For an overall design, you can section the background with border row stitches and then fill in with vignettes of individual and composite stitches.

Solid Fabric

Make a Wish

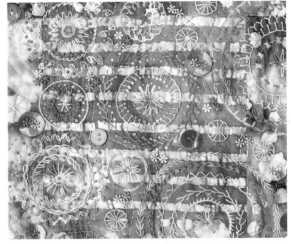

Detail of *Psychedelic Balloons* (page 41)

A wholecloth base offers endless possibilities for a design; this can be a solid color or a subtle batik. The embroidery pattern can be worked over a single template shape (such as a fan) or by repeating the motif (such as a circle) in various sizes from large to medium to small.

Printed Fabric

Square with stripes, checks, and polka dots

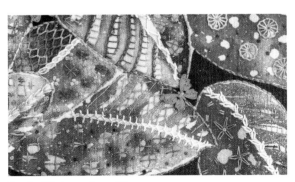

Detail of *Big Leaves* (page 22)

Fabrics with stripes, circles, or squares can be used as a guide for evenly spaced embroidery stitches. Printed fabrics that have a realistic pattern of waves, leaves, or flowers offer many possibilities for embroidery.

PIECED PATTERNS

The embroidery design on a pieced base can be worked on one or both sides of the seam or straddling the seam; the stitches can also be worked into the open spaces between seams. The length of the seam and the section of fabric between the adjacent seams will determine the size of the embroidered row and any additional stitched components.

Strip Pieced

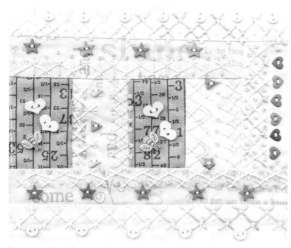

Square with strip-pieced sections

The pattern of a strip-pieced base design can have rows in equal or varied widths and lengths. The spacing between seams and the width and length of the row will help to determine the size and weight of the stitches.

Quilt Block

Square with appliqué pattern

A traditional quilt pattern can be used as a base, offering a realistic design to embroider around. The embroidery stitches and any additional components such as buttons or charms will further enhance the design.

Crazy Pieced

Square with crazy quilt piecing

A crazy-pieced base is just that: The fabrics are not even in size, shape, or length, thus the embroidery stitches are worked in size according to the spaces between the seamlines. Little vignettes can be worked into open spaces or corners and can be used to break up a long seam.

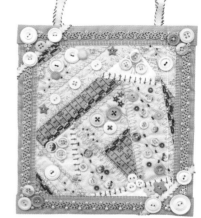

Scrappy Bits of Bark Chips and Stone

EMBELLISHMENT EXTRAS

Once the base of the project is designed, pieces of trim, ribbon, bits of lace, or appliqués can be added for additional design opportunities. The embroidery can be worked on the edges or through the width of the trim or lace, with the same stitch or with different stitches.

Flat Lace, Trims, and Ribbons

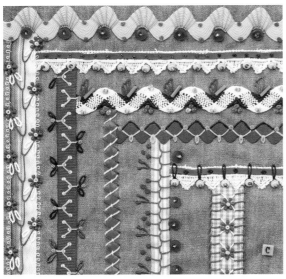

Square with ribbon and trims

Appliqués

Square with appliqués, buttons, and beads

Lengths of trim, ribbon, or lace can be used to create a design on a wholecloth base or to further enhance a strip- or crazy-pieced base. The embroidery design can be worked around, throughout, or over the edges of these components.

A wholecloth or pieced base can be stitched with a large appliqué or several small appliqués. The embroidery design can be worked around or over the edges of the appliqués and throughout the base.

Tips

- Temporarily glue a piece of lace, ribbon, trim, or appliqué with fabric glue; then hand stitch in place.

- When working a border row stitch with a tip, the edge of the stitch next to the shape will be shorter, and the tip will fan out.

- Work straight edges with individual or continuous stitches; work curves and dips with individual or composite stitches that can adapt to those shapes.

SPECIALTY APPLICATIONS

Embroidery stitches can be worked around the outline of a shape, within the shape, or to follow and increase the size of a shape. The stitches can fill in an entire section of the base or attach objects such as buttons and found objects.

Outlining a Shape

A border row stitch or repeated individual stitch can outline a drawn shape, such as a letter, or be stitched around a pattern or print in the fabric. The size of the shape will determine the size and type of the embroidery stitch.

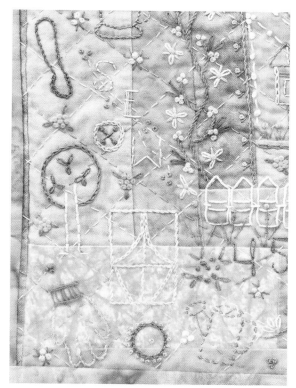

Detail of *Darling Motif Sampler* (page 31)

Netted and Laced Stitches

Embroidery stitches can fill in a section with a repeated design.

An individual or continuous stitch can be repeated across a row to create a netted design. A border row can be stitched and then laced or whipped with a different thread to create a broader row.

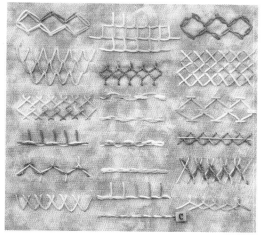

Square with netted, laced, and whipped stitches

Buttons

Embroidery stitches can be used to attach buttons and to create design interest. Sew the button in place with perle cotton; then add in any additional stitches.

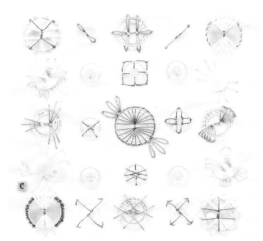

Square with buttons

Autumn Squared, a work in progress

WHAT, WHERE, WHEN

An embroidered project can have one type and weight of thread or several types of threads and weights; beads can be added in for extra details. Here are some examples of how to combine these components.

EMBROIDERED ROWS

Border row stitches	Decorative stitches	Detail stitches	Beaded stitches
Choice 1			
Perle cotton #5	Perle cotton #8	Perle cotton #12	Size 6°, 8° and/or 11° seed beads
Choice 2			
Perle cotton #5	Perle cotton #8	3 strands cotton floss	Size 6°, 8° and/or 11° seed beads
Choice 3			
Perle cotton #8	Perle cotton #12	3 strands cotton floss	Size 6°, 8° and/or 11° seed beads

The examples below show you two sections—both have the embroidery stitches worked in perle cotton #5, #8, and #12 and 3 strands of floss. The second section has size 6°, 8°, and 11° seed beads added.

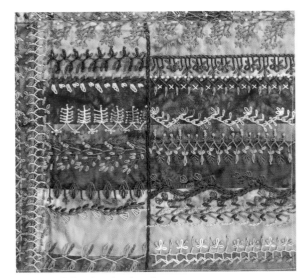

Close-up of all-embroidered section

Close-up of all-embroidered section with beads added

Tools, Tips, and Tricks

TOOLS AND GADGETS

1. 6″ clear quilters ruler (to mark lines for embroidery)

2. Awl or small crochet hook (to take out knots in thread or to remove cut threads)

3. Bead scoop or teaspoon (to pick up loose beads)

4. Dritz or Clover Seam Gauge (to gauge and compare the length of the embroidery stitches)

5. Erasable pen: air or water (to mark lines or template designs)

6. Found objects (to mark shapes for embroidery)

7. Fray Check (to treat raw edges)

8. Full-spectrum light (*not shown*)

9. Glue stick (to temporarily hold items in place)

10. Lightbox (*not shown*)

11. Needles: beading, chenille, cotton darner, crewel, embroidery, milliners, and sharps

12. Needle Puller (for thick fabrics and threads)

13. Needle threader

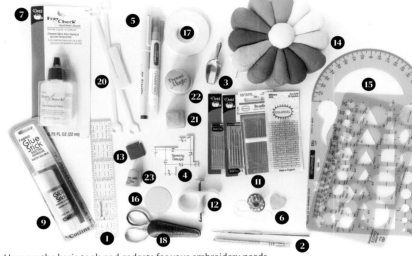

Here are the basic tools and gadgets for your embroidery needs.

14. Pincushion

15. Plastic templates (to use as an outline for a shape)

16. Rubber needle grabber (to pull the needle through layers of fabric)

17. ¼″ Quilter's Tape (to mark the shape and length of stitches)

18. Scissors: embroidery

19. Segmented bead dish (*not shown*)

20. StitchBow Floss Holder organizers (to keep floss from tangling)

21. Synthetic beeswax (to keep beading threads together)

22. Thread Magic conditioner (to minimize knotting of embroidery and sewing threads)

23. Thimble

24. Sewing Needle Pocket Guide for Hand Stitching, by Laura Wasilowski (to figure out what the loose needles in your stash are)

THE CORRECT NEEDLE

Tip To keep your needles organized, write each type of needle into a section of a tomato pincushion.

The purpose of the needle is to make a hole in the fabric big enough for the thread to pass through but not so big that the thread does not cover the hole. For needle sizes, the lower the number, the larger the needle.

- **Beading:** A thin short or long needle with a thin, long eye used for all types of beading threads

- **Chenille needle:** A medium-length needle with a long eye large enough for multiple threads

- **Cotton darner:** A long needle with an oval eye that is used for twisted threads

- **Crewel (also called an** *embroidery needle*): A medium-length needle with a medium-to-long eye that is wider than the shaft; used for twisted threads

- **Embroidery:** A fine, thin needle with a long eye that is used for stranded floss

- **Milliners:** A long needle with a small, rounded eye and a shaft the same width as the length of the needle; used for twisted threads and floss to embroider bullion knots

- **Sharps:** A shorter fine needle with a small eye; used for sewing thread and for beading

Tips for Threading the Needle

- Always cut the end of the thread straight across the grain.

- Pinch and/or wet the tip of the thread.

- Wet the eye of the needle; the moisture will attract the thread.

- Use a needle threader for floss or perle cotton.

- Try a magnifier glass with a light source.

- Hire a teenager who has great eyesight to thread your needles. (Don't laugh; I used to do this for a dear friend of mine!)

Knots

Once the needle is threaded, I knot the tail. After I work a row of stitches, I knot the thread on the wrong side and cut the thread. I then make a knot in the remaining thread, ready for the next row of stitches.

Instead, you could tack the thread at the beginning and end of a row. Make a tack stitch into the foundation of muslin or interfacing (not through the top layer). Take another tack stitch next to the first, pulling the thread to make a loop. Insert the needle through the loop and pull the knot closed.

WORKING WITH THE THREADS

The embroidery threads that you will be working with will either come wrapped in ball or twisted into a skein. The following specifics and tips will help you keep them tangle free and easy to use.

- Cut the embroidery threads and flosses 16"–18" (40.6cm–45.7cm) long.

- Cut the beading threads 1½ yards (1.4m) long; use double.

Perle Cotton

On a ball of perle cotton, you will find the loose end of thread wrapped horizontally around the ball and tucked under several layers of wrapped thread; pull gently to find the end. Thread the needle with the loose end, and then cut off the amount needed.

When working with a skein of perle cotton, first remove any paper wrappers or tags. Untwist the skein and find the knot. Then use one of the following suggestions to keep your threads tangle free.

- Cut the knot of thread and wrap the length of the skein over a StitchBow Floss Holder (see Tools, page 153). Place the wrapper with the color number on the small rectangular portion of the holder.

- Or cut through the entire skein at the knot. Make a loose knot to hold the threads together. Pull one thread out from the knot at a time, and cut the length into 2 pieces.

Stranded Floss

The mystery is always finding the tail without creating a big ball of knots. In most cases, the tail closest to the paper wrapper listing the color number will come out of the skein easily with no snarls.

Another option is to remove both of the paper wrappers from the skein and slip the skein over a StitchBow Floss Holder (see Tools, page 153). Tie the inner loose end to the loop on the StitchBow and place the wrapper with the color number on the small rectangular portion of the holder.

SPLITTING STRANDS OF FLOSS

In most cases you will be working with a portion of the 6-strand skein of floss. The number of strands you will use is up to you and your design.

1. Cut 18" (45.7cm) off the skein; split the threads into the number you need.

2. Hold the number of threads you need with one hand, between your thumb and forefinger.

3. Hold the remaining threads in the other hand, between your forefinger and middle finger.

4. Hold the length loosely between your thumb and ring finger.

5. Pull your hands apart slowly to release the strands from the skein, letting the thread flow between your thumb and ring finger.

6. Then separate each thread from this group and reassemble these back together to eliminate tangling.

Blending Threads

A few of the stitches will use 2 or more colors of thread. These threads are combined into one needle to create a unique color and texture to an embroidered stitch. Cut a longer length than you would normally use for a single strand of thread.

MAGIC STITCHES

Perle cotton: Cut 2 colors of the same size of thread, combine the lengths, and thread these into a cotton darner or crewel needle. Knot the ends together.

WHIP STITCHES

Perle cotton: Cut 2 or 3 colors of thread in the same size or a combination of sizes, combine the lengths, and thread these into a chenille needle. Knot the ends together.

Cotton floss: Cut 2 or 3 colors of thread, and separate 1 or more strands from each length. Combine the lengths and thread these into an embroidery needle. Knot the ends together. If you are using more than 1 strand for each color, then switch to a cotton darner or crewel needle.

Beading Threads and Waxing

Place the eye of the needle next to the wax, and pull the thread firmly over the wax. Place the eye of the needle at your forefinger, and close your thumb over the thread. Pull the thread through your fingers to merge the 2 threads.

Tips for Taming the Threads

I keep a piece of cardboard with holes punched out to organize the unused portion of strands of floss. This way you will always be able to find the second half of the split skein.

All of the threads will naturally twist as you stitch; if you periodically hold the fabric base upside down, letting the thread and needle dangle down, the thread will unwind.

Run the length of twisted thread or floss over Thread Magic to prevent the tail of the thread from knotting or wrapping around the working portion of the thread.

The end of the thread that is threaded through the needle should periodically be cut, as it becomes frayed while you are stitching, and it can cause knots to occur when it wraps around the working thread.

Most hand-dyed threads are colorfast, however pre-testing a sample by hand washing it is always a good idea.

Keep the threads clean and dust free by storing them in a bag with a ziplock closure. I have a separate bag for each project and a smaller bag for the leftover odds and ends. You may never know when you need just a few inches to finish off a stitch.

GETTING YOUR PROJECTS ORGANIZED

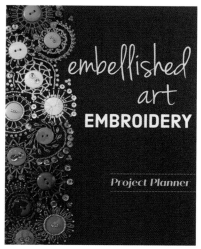

Embellished Art Embroidery Project Planner

I find that I don't work on just one project at a time, and I need a way to keep track of all of the projects that I am working on. This project planner allows me to this while providing a year at a glance for all of my creative goals.

During the design phase of each project, I store the materials and other components in a bag or small box. I clip a swatch of all the fabrics, threads, and trims and place these in the planner. I also include any drawings or design ideas that I want to include in the creation.

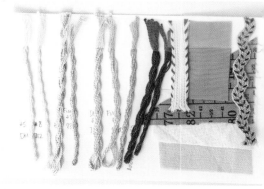

Fabric and thread sample index card

For each project, I also keep an index card, which includes a swatch of the fabrics and a small section of each thread with the name and color number of the thread listed. This way if I need to buy more, I can take my swatch card with me to the store.

I jot down the stitches that I am using on a project and keep this record with the threads. This way if I have to leave a project to work on another, I can refer to my notes for the number of wraps for a French knot or how many strands of floss that I used.

EXPERIENCES SHARED FROM THE FIELD

- Always wash your hands before working with the fabrics and threads.

- Prewash fabrics to remove chemicals and accumulated dust.

- Serge or zigzag the outer raw edges of the fabric base to prevent fraying while you work the stitches.

- Use Fray Check to help keep lace, ribbons and trims from fraying. I also apply a thin layer to the edges of my fabric base when working with a loose weave.

- Use a fabric glue stick to temporarily keep lace, ribbons, and trims in place while stitching.

- Think of a mistake as a design opportunity that you had not thought of yet. Once you repeat a mistake, it becomes another element in the design.

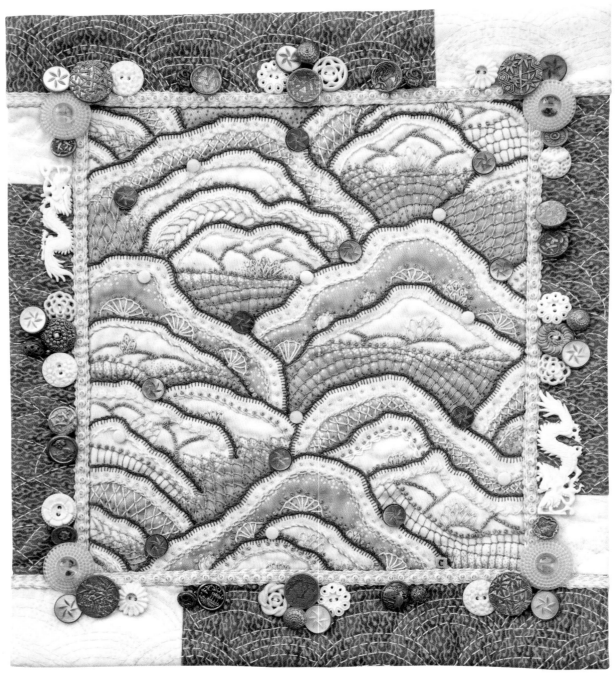

Misty Blue Hills

Bibliography

Gentle Lady's Needle Keep

Felt Needle Keep and Thimble Holder. This group was embroidered with hand-dyed perle cotton threads from Artfabrik by Laura Wasilowski.

Bond, Dorothy. *Crazy Quilt Stitches*: Dorothy Bond, 1981.

Enthoven, Jacqueline. *The Stitches of Creative Embroidery*, New York: Van Nostrand Reinhold, 1964.

John, Edith. *Creative Stitches*, Mineola, NY: Dover Publications, 1973.

Montano, Judith Baker. *Judith Baker Montano's Embroidery & Crazy Quilt Stitch Tool*, Lafayette, CA: C&T Publishing, 2008.

Petersen, Grete, Elsie Svennas, Anne Wilkins. *Handbook of Stitches*, New York: Van Nostrand Reinhold, 1970.

Thomas, Mary, Jan Eaton. *Mary Thomas's Dictionary of Embroidery Stitches*, North Pomfret, VT: Trafalgar Square Publishing, 2001.

Wilson, Erica. *Erica Wilson's Embroidery Book*, New York: Charles Scribner's Sons, 1973

About the Author

Christen Brown was born in Manhattan Beach, California, and spent her formative years in Torrance, California. She first became interested in fiber arts when she began making clothing for her dolls as a child. After graduating from high school, she continued her education at the Fashion Institute of Design & Merchandising in Los Angeles, California, where she graduated with an associate of arts in fashion design.

Christen began her career in the wearable art field in 1986. Her work has been shown in galleries and fashion shows all over the world. She has been invited to participate in both the Fairfield and BERNINA Fashion Shows. She has had her work included in *The Costume-Maker's Art*, *The Button Craft Book*, *Michaels Arts & Crafts* magazine, *Martha Stewart Weddings* magazine, and *Visions: Quilts of a New Decade* (by C&T Publishing). She has written a human-interest article for *Threads* magazine and has had several historical articles published by *Piecework* magazine.

Christen began teaching and presenting her work in 1991. She has taught for quilt and fiber art guilds on the west coast, and she has been invited to teach nationally for Road to California, American Quilter's Society, and the International Quilt Festival.

Christen's published titles for C&T Publishing include *Ribbonwork Gardens*, *Embroidered & Embellished*, *Ribbonwork Flowers*, *The Embroidery Book*, *Embroidery Stitching Handy Pocket Guide*, *Beaded Embroidery Stitching*, and *Embellished Art Embroidery Project Planner*. She also designed two sets of templates, Embroidery Stencils: Essential Collection and Embroidery Stencils: Darling Motif Collection.

Christen continues to be interested in craft and fine art and to experiment and learn all that she can, specifically concentrating on design and the techniques of embroidery, quilting, ribbonwork, mixed media, and beadwork. Her goal and wish through this journey is to continually be surprised, inspired, and creative, and to be necessary.

....

Visit Christen online!

Website: christenbrown.com

Blog: christenbrown.com/blog

Facebook: /christenjbrown

Pinterest: /christenjbrown

....

Also by Christen Brown:

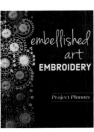